First edition published October 2019

Oftwominds.com
P.O. Box 4727
Berkeley, California 94704

Interior: Jill Kanter
Cover: Theresa Barzyk
Cover concept: G.F.B.

With gratitude to Richard Metzger for suggesting I turn an essay on this topic into a book; to Michael Meusel for the quote that begins this book; to Simons Chase for sharing his concept of negative network effects; to my friends Steve and Clara who are living the values presented here, and to Cindy for listening and consulting as I struggled to bring all these ideas to the page.

Will You Be Richer or Poorer? Profit, Power and A.I. in a Traumatized World

Charles Hugh Smith

Table of Contents

Section One: What Is Wealth?

Will you be richer or poorer in the future? Will the world be richer or poorer?

These questions are deceptively simple. Based on conventional financial measures, the answer seems straightforward: yes, you'll be richer, and so will the world, as consumption, income and wealth all continue trending higher.

But there's more to wealth than dollars, euros, yen or yuan, or ounces of gold.

The Problem with Measuring Wealth

Many types of wealth can't be reduced to tidy dollar amounts, and others can't be measured with conventional financial metrics. As author Daniel Yankelovich observed in 1972 (*Corporate Priorities: A continuing study of the new demands on business*):

> *"The first step is to measure whatever can be easily measured. This is OK as far as it goes.*
>
> *The second step is to disregard that which can't be easily measured or to give it an arbitrary quantitative value. This is artificial and misleading.*
>
> *The third step is to presume that what can't be measured easily really isn't important. This is blindness.*
>
> *The fourth step is to say that what can't be easily measured really doesn't exist. This is suicide."*

This describes the problem with measuring wealth only in monetary units: we disregard or assign arbitrary and misleading numbers to types of *societal capital* such as clean air and water, and we presume that what can't be easily measured—*intangible capital*—isn't important, when it may actually be more important than whatever *can* be measured in dollars. And lastly, since we don't even recognize many forms of intangible capital, they simply don't exist in our narratives of how the world works.

In other words, our conventional way of measuring wealth is blind - and potentially suicidal.

There's another problem with conventional measures of wealth: they become powerful incentives to rig statistics in order to generate a politically appealing illusion of financial advancement, even as wealth measured in broader terms may be declining.

(While the markers of wealth vary by culture, the economic measures of gross domestic product (GDP), income, unemployment, etc. and social measures such as child mortality rates, social mobility, etc. are standards applied to all national economies. For the purposes of this discussion, *wealth* includes all types of capital and *well-being*, while *prosperity* considers the distribution of wealth: is a rising tide raising all boats, or is the elite gaining ground while everyone else is losing ground? Even if they're statistically wealthier than people in other nations, the populace losing ground will feel less prosperous.)

But there's an even deeper problem with conventional measures of wealth: the way we measure *profit*, the ultimate incentive to human endeavor, is profoundly flawed. As a result, even our bedrock financial measurements are, in Yankelovich's term, *artificial and misleading*.

The goal of this book is to examine all forms of wealth and well-being, and look critically at the conventional financial measures, before answering the question, *are we getting richer or poorer?*

Factors Contributing to Diminishing Wealth

While conventional measures of wealth such as GDP, income and net worth are lofting ever higher in most nations, by other measures the world is traumatized by staggering losses and rising insecurity.

- Consider nations choking on industrial air pollution. How wealthy are the financially well-off in such nations if they breathe toxic air and can't drink tap water? Isn't toxic air and water a form of impoverishment? How much is their financial wealth worth if it can't provide clean air and water? Social wealth—the results of social structures, values and investments—may well be a more important measure of wealth in terms of well-being than individual financial wealth.
- It's well-known that pollinating insects are in decline due to human pollution and overuse of pesticides and other chemicals. As insect populations crash, this threatens humanity's harvests from sources that require pollination by these insects. How is a reduction in food supply not a form of impoverishment? Does this diminishment of global wealth appear on any financial balance sheets? No, because the impact isn't easily measured, and there are powerful political and financial incentives to ignore anything which might diminish the perceived expansion of prosperity. While food production may still be rising, the increasing fragility of that production is ignored because it calls the narrative of permanently higher yields into question.
- Human overuse of antibiotics in animal husbandry and healthcare is creating *superbugs*, bacteria that are resistant to all conventional antibiotics. Humanity is in effect breeding new and deadly diseases that may ultimately threaten much of humanity. How is the emergence of untreatable bacterial diseases not a diminishment of global wealth?

To truly measure wealth, we need to focus on all that is not measured by purely financial metrics—social, human, natural and intangible capital.

Measuring Intangible Wealth

On a corporate level, a conventional financial example of *intangible capital* includes corporate brands and customer loyalty to those brands. The capital is intangible but it has real-world results on sales and profits.

As well, a society's intangible capital includes, among many other things, cultural heritage and trust in institutions. This capital is intangible but the loss of heritage and trust in institutions has real-world consequences. Greece offers a recent example of a systemic financial crisis leading to a loss of trust in institutions.

A household's intangible capital includes, among many other things, financial security. If the household wealth is at the whim of volatile financial booms and busts, then how secure is the wealth? Clearly, there can be no sustainable financial security when wealth that balloons up in a bubble vanishes just as quickly in the inevitable bust.

This book will examine wealth in terms of *sustainable well-being*—health, safety, longevity, security, social mobility, trust, liberty, positive social roles, etc., as well as the conventional financial terms of income and ownership of capital. We will also examine access to wealth extracted from the Earth and its natural systems—energy, fresh water and nutrient-rich foods—because financial wealth that can't be converted into well-being is of limited value, regardless of its magnitude in financial terms.

Wealth: The Accumulation of Capital

Historically, wealth is measured by the *accumulation of productive capital*: civilizations that accumulate productive capital (roads, shipping, metalworking, beneficial agricultural tools and techniques, stable institutions of governance and security, etc.), becoming wealthier as the gains enabled by these capital improvements continue accumulating.

The same is true of private wealth: households became wealthier by acquiring more land and working it more effectively with better, more productive tools and techniques, and then using the improved roads to move their surplus to markets where they could fetch the best prices.

We can divide this *productive wealth* into *societal* and *private* wealth.

- *Societal wealth* is available to everyone, a form of *the Commons*, assets held by the community, state or empire for the general use of all inhabitants. This is *publicly beneficial capital*.
- *Private wealth* is held by individuals, families, institutions such as guilds, religious groups, and so on—wealth that generates returns primarily for the owners and secondarily to society at large in the form of goods and services which can be purchased from the owners of productive capital.

If we ask the general public *what is wealth,* the typical answer would focus on *consumption wealth*: comfort, convenience and luxury goods that confer high social status. How the wealth is produced is generally of less interest than how it is spent. This focus is natural in an economy that's dominated by consumer marketing and spending.

There's a contradiction in this mix of production and consumption: accumulating the productive capital that generates wealth requires sacrificing consumption in favor of saving and determined effort, both of which run counter to consumption's demands to spend freely and devote as much time to leisure as possible.

This brief outline highlights some basic truths about wealth. A society that doesn't save capital and invest those savings in productive capital will soon consume its wealth and become poorer. This is *scale-invariant*, meaning that it is equally true of empires and households alike.

A society that doesn't accumulate capital that benefits everyone while enabling the unlimited expansion of private productive capital becomes an asymmetric society of a small class of very wealthy owners of capital and a mass of laborer-consumers who own little productive capital and are thus poor.

If capital is invested in private palaces and temples, for example, rather than in public roadways, secure trading routes, and so on—*publicly beneficial capital*—the majority will be poor for two reasons: they own little productive capital, and in such a capital-poor society they lack the means to earn enough money to save and invest in productive capital.

The relative wealth or poverty of the majority is largely influenced by the organization of trade and markets. If the society is dominated by *captive markets* (markets controlled by a monopoly or cartel) and limited trade routes and trade volumes, the society is commonly characterized by mass poverty. Not only is the ownership of productive capital limited, so is access to the goods and services being produced.

An example of a captive market is a forest owned by the nobility for its own use. The forest may have plenty of resources desired by the peasantry—fallen wood, wild game, etc.—but the majority have no access to the resources, even if they have the means to purchase them.

An *open market*, in contrast, enables the free trade of goods and services between all participants: those who own the productive capital, laborers selling their labor, traders taking advantage of local scarcities and surpluses, and so on. An open market benefits from multiple trade routes and a high volume of tradable goods.

But ownership of productive capital is only half the picture. The other half is the *accessibility* of the goods and services produced by that capital by the majority.

Characteristics of Wealthy vs. Poor Societies

A society in which most of the productive capital is owned by a handful of wealthy families and companies can generate widely accessible wealth for all inhabitants if most of the private wealth is invested in publicly beneficial capital such as free transportation routes, public health measures such as clean water, open markets for goods and labor, access to credit, secure trade routes and so on.

If this society also nurtures a culture of competent governance, general security (legal protection of private property, defined rights of employers and employees, etc.) and social mobility (i.e. anyone can better themselves, no matter how lowly their initial status in society), then this *cultural capital* will greatly increase the accessibility of publicly beneficial capital.

All of these publicly beneficial forms of capital characterize the early Roman Republic and Empire: secure travel and trade routes, open markets, reasonably competent governance, broad accessibility to public capital (clean water, public baths, markets, and forums) and defined citizens' rights along with many forms of social mobility.

Alternatively, societies characterized by wealth that is hoarded by a tiny class of ruling elites (e.g. gold stored in the vaults of palaces, resources reserved exclusively for the elite, little capital invested in publicly beneficial assets) are-captive markets with poor security, little trade, low social mobility and uneven governance are poor.

Historically, the *natural capital* of a region plays an essential role in the wealth or poverty of a society. Natural capital includes the resources that can be harvested, mined or extracted such as forests, metal ores, coal and fresh water, as well as the predominant weather patterns, fertility of the soils, the geography of rivers and valleys that make trade easy or difficult, and so on. Even the diversity of micro-climates within the region is a form of capital, as greater diversity enables specialized crops and beneficial trading within the region.

History offers many examples of societies that depleted their natural capital and then collapsed once they consumed their inherited natural wealth. Depletion of soils and energy sources often leads to warfare and the spread of disease once inhabitants no longer have enough food to keep healthy, and ruling elites seek to conquer the remaining resources of nearby polities to maintain their own consumption.

Fluctuations in weather, trade, and climate can exacerbate depletion by spreading new pathogens to populations that lack immunity, reducing crop yields.

Societies dependent on high levels of natural resource extraction often falter when depletion leads to declines that cannot be compensated with imports or substitutions. There are no substitutes when rainfall declines, forests have been chopped down, and mines are depleted.

Much of what we perceive as *human-generated wealth* is actually our *inherited natural capital* being consumed. Sustainability of a society's consumption of natural capital is thus a critical factor when measuring wealth: if natural capital is declining, this fact alone will offset any gains made in financial capital. Not only can non-renewable resources be depleted, but even renewable resources such as fisheries and forests can be destroyed by over-use.

Surpluses extracted from natural capital can be traded for gold, but once natural capital is depleted, there are no surpluses left to trade. A hoard of gold may be able to buy grain for a season or two, but no amount of gold can reverse long-term drought, renew depleted soil or conjure up resources that has been consumed.

If a society is spending its natural capital at an accelerating rate, the consumption of what cannot be replaced generates a temporary illusion of wealth. If the ledger of wealth includes natural capital that's being depleted, then the society may be becoming poorer even as it revels in a last dying splurge of overconsumption—in effect, fiddling while Rome burns.

If a society is consuming more than it sustainably produces, it is becoming poorer, regardless of the financial illusions of wealth generated by consumption. If their productive capital is eroding, regardless of the cause (depletion, overconsumption, etc.), impoverishment is the inevitable result. Conversely, societies that are accumulating *sustainably productive capital* are becoming richer.

External Costs: What Markets Don't Include in Price

External costs refer to costs of production that are borne not by the producer but by the society at large. Examples include industrial production that pollutes the air and water, planned obsolescence that generates waste that society must pay to recycle or dispose of, and the eventual cost of replacing what was depleted. For example, once the fisheries have been wiped out, the costs of finding replacement sources of protein fall on consumers and society, not those who reaped the gain from overfishing.

Though external costs are traditionally limited to physical effects such as pollution, the intangible distortions created by those maximizing their private gains in ways that cost society at large can also be viewed as external costs. For example, the mortgage lending sector reaped enormous profits from packaging and selling subprime mortgages as low-risk financial assets in the early 2000's, but the economic fallout from this fraudulent exploitation ended up costing society in numerous ways, both tangible (loss of homes) and intangible (loss of confidence in institutions).

When external costs are paid by society at large, *profits are private but losses are public*. If we total the private profits and the much greater losses of public capital resulting from the mortgage meltdown, it's clear that the profits were *systemically illusory*: taken as a whole, the entire speculative mortgage-housing bubble created far more losses than it did gains, especially if we add the decline in interest income earned by savers as central banks cut rates to near-zero to boost housing sales.

Such a bubble dynamic creates temporary illusions of wealth that soon dissipate once the external costs manifest—for example, the housing bubble, sparked by an explosion in speculative mortgage lending, created a brief illusion of wealth for home buyers that was shattered when the bubble burst.

Before the external costs are tallied, the wealth captured by speculators lends a sheen of rising wealth to the society as a whole, even if the majority of gains are flowing to a tiny minority. But this sheen is also temporary, since paying the external costs reduces public capital. As a few reap immense profits by transferring external costs to society, society becomes poorer: if we measure the gain or loss in total capital, the perceived profit is illusory for but the speculators who cashed out at the top.

This reality is masked by the widely accepted but false belief that markets price in all costs. In reality, markets lack the mechanisms to do anything more than include the immediate costs of production, processing and distribution. As a result, they are incapable of pricing in external costs and losses in natural capital such as the decline in biodiversity. This will be discussed in detail in a subsequent section.

As an example, consider a fishing expedition that strip-mines the seas with nets and uses dynamite to indiscriminately kill fish in shallow water. Only the fish with market value are cleaned, cooled and sent on to market. But since much of the wildlife captured by these means have little to no market value, most of the dead fish are dumped back into the ocean after sorting.

The immediate costs incurred by harvesting the marketable fish are easily calculated: wages for the crew, fuel for the boat, maintenance of the nets, ice to cool the fish, and transport to market. But the *full* costs of this method of fishing cannot readily be calculated, much less included in the market price. What price do we place on the ecosystem that's been destroyed by the dynamite, and the food chain decimated by overfishing? How can the loss of natural capital possibly be fully measured?

As Daniel Yankelovich explained, assigning arbitrary quantitative values to what cannot be easily measured is misleading, and ignoring what cannot be easily measured is suicide.

If we only measure the immediate costs of overfishing and the market price of the few fish humans pay a premium to consume, we appear to be getting richer. But this modest gain is dwarfed by the loss of capital caused by overfishing. Just because we can't easily measure this loss doesn't mean it isn't occurring. Rather, the market's incomplete *discovery* of cost lead us to believe that we're accumulating gains rather than suffering catastrophic losses of natural capital.

This false accounting leads to decisions that are suicidal because what cannot be easily measured is assumed not to exist.

The Limits of Measuring Capital and Wealth

Humans *optimize what we measure* and discount what we don't measure. Once gain and loss are tied to a measurement, we focus not just on the measure per se but on the value leveraged by the measurement. Employees optimize *what they get measured on*, to increase their financial gain, and ignore what they aren't measured on.

Since we measure financial transactions embedded in markets (buying or selling labor, goods and services, loaning money, and so on), we try to optimize our financial gain and reduce our losses.

Since we do not measure anything that cannot be measured as easily as financial transactions (e.g. external costs and other losses of capital), we have no real grasp of whether we're accumulating capital (getting richer) or losing capital (getting poorer). This includes both tangible forms of capital such as ecosystems and highways and intangible forms of capital: *human capital* (our skills, knowledge and experience); *social capital* (the value of our social connections and networks); and *cultural capital* (formal institutions, value systems, cultural heritage, willingness to trust fellow citizens, etc.). These are difficult to measure so they don't get measured.

Measuring Natural Capital

Natural capital is difficult to quantify due to what's not readily visible: the nutrients in the soil, remaining reserves of minerals, etc. It may be impossible to accurately measure the loss of biodiversity because species that were never identified may have already gone extinct. Since trees, animals, bacteria, fungi, and other micro-organisms are all potential sources for novel medicines, the loss of biodiversity could be incalculable in terms of human suffering that could have been alleviated had we preserved ecosystems intact rather than laying waste to them to extract whatever parts are currently valued by markets.

Measuring Tangible Capital

Tangible capital is complicated to calculate for a variety of reasons relating to the type of capital being measured. For example, tangible public capital such as bridges and roadways pose difficulties due to the *opportunity costs* embedded in every capital expenditure: what else of greater value could this capital have been invested in? Investing in *bridges to nowhere* may generate short-term financial gains such as jobs and orders for concrete and steel, but what else could that labor, concrete, and steel have constructed that would have been of greater value to society at large? Such questions may appear abstract or even political in nature, but if we understand that *capital is not infinite* and *value flows to what's scarce*, then addressing scarcities (or proactively avoiding creating scarcities) is inherently a more valuable use of capital than building lightly used bridges.

Measuring Intangible Capital

The difficulties in quantifying capital accumulation or loss become even greater in the realm of intangible capital. We'll examine intangible capital in depth in a later section, but we can start by listing forms of intangible capital: well-being; trust in institutions; trust in one's fellow citizens; cultural heritage; positive social roles; social mobility; personal agency, and control of one's own human and financial capital. In many cases, we take these for granted, and have difficulty even recognizing them as important forms of capital.

As consumers, we're inundated with claims extolling the value of convenience, which covers everything from frozen meals, labor-saving devices, goods delivered to our door, online services that automate some aspect of our increasingly complex lives, etc.

Marketing attempts to persuade us that convenience and status are wealth. The motivation is obvious: if we trade capital for convenience, the purveyors of convenience reap profits. What marketing studiously ignores is the opportunity cost of convenience and status: what else could we have invested our capital in that generated more value?

Put another way: are we actually getting poorer while marketers tell us we're getting richer? Marketers reap profits by conflating *needs and wants*: our basic needs (referring to Maslow's *Hierarchy of Needs*) are few, while our wants are many. *You can have it all* is the motto of marketers, where *having it all* refers to profitable goods and services. But if we tune out the ubiquitous marketing and focus on recognizing and measuring our *productive intangible capital*, we'll end up with a more complex and accurate sense of whether we're accumulating or losing capital, i.e. becoming richer or poorer.

Section Two: Will Technology Make Us All Richer?

This section examines what many propose is the new wellspring of wealth, the automation technologies of robotics and artificial intelligence (AI), which many believe will generate so much wealth that all 7.5 billion humans currently on the planet will benefit not only materially, but by being freed from work. Examining these claims will illuminate the flaws in our understanding, not just of wealth, but of how our economy actually works.

If new information leads to a conclusion we don't want to hear, we tend to find ways to dismiss the new information. If we benefit from the status quo, our natural bias will be to dismiss any information which undermines our faith that the status quo and economic growth are permanent.

Thus there is a constant battle between our innate biases against information that leads to conclusions we don't want to deal with, versus our awareness that realistic assessments are necessary for survival. In this section I'll challenge the core beliefs underpinning the expectations that profits from automation will enrich all of humanity far into the future. I ask that you follow the results to their logical conclusions.

Will Robotics and AI Be Immensely Profitable?

It's now widely accepted that robots and artificial intelligence (AI) will displace tens of millions of human workers; in fact, many observers foresee the eventual replacement of most human labor.

The problem created by this forecast is obvious: if workers lose their jobs, how will they get the income needed to live?

Two Scenarios

There are two camps of thought. The first holds that technology has always created more and better jobs than it destroys, and this will continue to be the case. The second holds that this wave of automation will destroy far more jobs than it creates, but the solution is to *tax the robots* and use these revenues to distribute the wealth to everyone who no longer has a livelihood.

Both cases assume we'll get richer: if technology generates more high-quality jobs, replacing lower-quality jobs lost to automation, we'll collectively get richer; conversely, if technology destroys jobs but creates immense profits that can be distributed to everyone as Universal Basic Income (UBI), then we'll get richer via distribution of profits to everyone.

But what if neither option is realistic? What if the new jobs that are created in the wake of automation are lower-quality, lower pay, and far more insecure? And what if automation leads to much lower profits rather than much higher profits? What if there's nowhere near enough profits to distribute to everyone as Universal Basic Income? If that's the case, we're collectively becoming poorer, even if a small percentage of the population is reaping wealth from automation.

Taxing the robots is intuitively appealing. If the enterprises employing robots and AI will generate immense profits that society can tax to fund UBI, this will provide an income for everyone who no longer has paid work.

But what if the enterprises employing robots and AI will never be very profitable due to the mechanics of *commoditization*? If UBI can't be funded with taxes on profits, then how many paying customers will these automated enterprises have if tens of millions of households no longer have a secure income?

The profitability of robots and AI is thus critical to our question, *will we be richer or poorer?*

The Need for Profits

Let's start by understanding that profits are required in every socio-economic system. Even a socialist economy in which the state owns all the major enterprises must generate profits to fund its social welfare programs. Absent profits, social welfare programs must be paid for by borrowing or printing money, neither of which is sustainable in the long run.

But profits are not guaranteed. Paraphrasing author Peter Drucker, *enterprises don't have profits, they only have costs*. In other words, profits are not inevitable, only costs are inevitable, and this is as true of state-owned enterprises as it is for private-sector enterprises.

All enterprises, both private and government owned, must generate profits to fund capital expenditures (replacing worn out equipment, etc.), overhead (management, utilities, accounting, etc.) and dividends to the owners in return for their investment.

If enterprises owned by the state lose money every month, they must be subsidized by other taxpayers. If all state-owned enterprises are unprofitable, eventually the state itself becomes insolvent.

How do enterprises make money with robots and software? Technologies become profitable by reducing costs and increasing productivity, i.e. creating more goods and services with the same number of workers and same amount of capital investment. Since labor (known as *labor inputs*) is a primary expense along with production and overhead, automation becomes profitable when it replaces human labor with cheaper automation and/or increases the productivity of the remaining workers.

Since technology increases profits by reducing costs and increasing productivity, and the costs of labor are increasing globally, replacing human employees with automation is the obvious way to reduce costs and boost profits.

To take an example from the 20th century, if a factory replaces 100 assembly-line employees with robots, and needs only ten employees to oversee and maintain the robots, it will increase profits if the cost of buying and operating the robots is lower than the cost of human labor. If the robots can produce more goods and services than human employees, profits will also increase due to higher productivity.

Replacing workers with automation is not optional, since competitors who do so can lower prices, reduce human errors and increase their market share. Employers are forced to replace human workers to compete with companies that have already lowered their costs by investing in automation.

Those reckoning automation will boost profits assume the price of the components being produced will remain stable. In the real world, price is set by supply and demand. Since automation tends to increase production, supply soon exceeds demand. To maintain sales, competitors lower prices. As prices spiral down, profit margins decline. (Since they have no competitors, monopolies can maintain high prices by artificially limiting supply.)

Proponents of the idea that robotics/AI will generate vast new wealth overlook the enormously deflationary impact of technology in general and of *commoditized* technology specifically: once robotics and AI become *commoditized* (i.e. the components and coding are interchangeable and available everywhere), if there are competitors in the market, costs drop as supply outpaces demand, and the prices of the finished goods and services also decline, reducing profits to razor-thin margins.

Globally, *over-capacity*—excess capacity to produce more goods and services—is now commonplace. Few enterprises have *pricing power*, i.e. the power to increase prices, because demand rarely exceeds supply for long, given global competition and over-capacity.

This is the story of commoditized manufacturing in China, where the vast majority of companies scrape by on extremely thin margins. Many of China's state-owned enterprises (SOEs) are unprofitable and must be subsidized to continue operations. Estimates of the wages and profits that remain in China from assembling an Apple iPhone find that only a thin sliver of the retail price of the phone flows to enterprises in China, roughly $8.50 out of a retail price of $650 and manufacturer's cost of $240.

Yes, Apple is profitable, but there is only one Apple. Manufacturers of commodity phones in China struggle to break even. This the result of commoditization, competition and over-capacity.

Marginal Costs and Scarcity Value

To understand why commoditization drives costs relentlessly lower, we have to understand *marginal costs* and *scarcity value* in the digital age.

Consider a mass-produced general-purpose semiconductor chip. The initial investment in the fabrication machinery is costly, and the first production run can be sold at a high prices due to its relative scarcity in the marketplace: the new chip is faster than previous chips, etc.

Value is a function of scarcity. What's *scarce and in demand* has more value than what is abundant.

The scarcity value of the new chip attracts competitors, and since the return on the initial investment has largely been recouped by initial sales, the original manufacturer can lower prices to maintain market share when competing chips come on the market.

Since most of the manufacturing is automated, the *labor inputs* per chip are very low. Once the machinery and software have been paid for, the marginal cost of production is far lower than it was at the start of production. The costs of continuing production have fallen to a relative handful of production workers and the overhead of utilities, rent, management and sales, etc.

The additional cost of producing one more chip is known as the *marginal cost*. Once the production equipment has been paid for, the marginal cost of producing an additional chip falls precipitously if the labor input (i.e. cost of the handful of production workers) per chip is low.

As a result, the marginal cost of producing the chip falls from $10 each to $1 each.

As competing chips are interchangeable and are produced at a number of plants around the world, the chip is a *commodity*, as opposed to a customized product for which there is no substitute. Once other companies are producing equivalent chips in volume, the *scarcity value* of the chip falls.

Where the first manufacturer could sell each chip for $15, a $5 profit per chip, once the chip becomes commoditized, its scarcity value plummets. The price might fall to $1.25 per unit, leaving the manufacturer with $.20 for overhead and a razor-thin profit of $.05 per unit.

Given that the factory only needs a handful of staff to keep the production line running, the labor input per chip has also declined. As a result, the only way to increase the profit margin is to reduce the expenses for overhead such as utilities, rent, management, marketing, taxes, etc.

Let's now turn to the marginal cost of software. Since open-source software is distributed freely and the cost of distribution of digital files is near-zero, as the cost of chips and software plummets, the price of the finished consumer devices also drops if there are competing manufacturers. This is why the wholesale price of commodity tablet computers with open-source software has declined to less than $40 each. As prices plummet, so do profit margins. This is why manufacturers of commodity smart phones in China struggle to break even despite selling millions of phones.

What keeps the components of automation and AI from being commoditized? Nothing. They are simply the latest technologies that will be commoditized. If there are global competitors, prices will decline as production ramps up, pushing profit margins to near-zero. Put another way: how are the components of automation and AI different from the many high-tech components in smart phones? If the profit margins on commoditized smart phones are near-zero, why won't the profit margins on automation and AI also trend to near-zero?

It's important to note that not all technology must be cutting edge to be useful to consumers. In most cases, the components need only be *good enough*. Beyond *good enough*, the value of the *latest and greatest* depends on the status value of the brand, not the utility.

Consider the memory in a computer. Due to commoditization of the components, the cost of memory has fallen to the point that very few consumers make use of the memory that's available on even the lowest-price computers. There is no reason for them to pay extra for even more memory they'll never use. The cheapest commoditized memory is good enough.

Very few applications require costly custom components; *good enough* meets consumer needs. So the scarcity value of much higher cost components is limited by narrow demand. Relatively few consumers globally are willing or able to pay a big premium for the *latest and greatest*. (Of the 94 million autos sold globally annually, fewer than 8 million are luxury brands, and Apple iPhones are less than 12% of the global smart phone market.)

As a general rule, system speed is limited to their slowest component, and so increasing the speed or efficiency of all components at a significant increase in cost rarely makes financial sense. When designing a complex system such as a smart phone, auto or robot, it makes financial sense to design the device around readily available, low-cost commodity components and open-source software rather than increase the cost by specifying custom parts or software that add little market value to the finished product. Indeed, the profit margins of manufacturers of complex technologies such as autos depend on keeping the costs of electronic components as low as possible.

As a result of these technical realities and financial incentives, robots are being commoditized as their components and software are commoditized. As with all commoditized technologies, over time the profit markets will decline to near-zero as competitors enter production.

As for AI: AI is software, and as such it is essentially free to duplicate and distribute. Software is also being commoditized, as libraries of coding and applications are available online for relatively nominal cost or for free. The scarcity value of *good enough* AI software is also falling rapidly.

If the history of technology is any guide—and there is no evidence that robotics and AI software are different from previous technologies—the profit margins on robotics, AI and automation will decline as their components are commoditized and competition increases production. Rather than being immensely profitable, the tools of automation will be commoditized and low-profit. *Taxing the robots* will yield very little in the way of taxes.

The Limits of Monopoly and Artificial Scarcity

But what about Apple, Google, Facebook, Twitter, Amazon, Microsoft, Uber, Alibaba and the other tech giants reaping billions in profits? Aren't they evidence that technology is immensely profitable?

To understand why so few companies are so profitable, we need to understand *monopoly* and *artificial scarcity*. When an enterprise holds a monopoly, it is the sole source of a good or service people want or need. This demand and the *artificial scarcity* generated by restricting the supply gives the monopoly *pricing power*, meaning the price they charge can be much higher than it would be if competing sources were available. The monopoly can thus command a premium reserved for scarce goods and services. This higher price translates into high profit margins.

When a handful of companies manage to limit supply to maintain artificial scarcity, this is known as a *cartel*. Enterprises in the cartel are nominally competitors, but the members artificially fix prices across the board; there isn't much difference in the prices charged by each member. Cartels can be formal like the Organization of Petroleum Exporting Countries (OPEC), or informal. In either case, the cartel serves to limit competition, ensuring restricted supply and high profits. (In the U.S. and other nations, there are laws against this sort of price-fixing, but it's difficult to prosecute if there are no records supporting the accusation.)

In terms of ensuring high profits, the ideal scenario in any market is monopoly or a cartel. Monopoly can be imposed by the government—government is itself a monopoly in many ways—or by private ownership (for example, Rockefeller's dominating ownership of oil in the early 20th century), or by establishing a dominant market position via a coveted brand or a *positive network effect*.

When every new user who joins a network adds value to the network itself, this is known as a *positive network effect*. Google's dominance in web search is an example: every person who started using Google for web searches made Google's marketing service more valuable, as there were more consumers who would see ads placed by advertisers. The more consumers who used Google, the greater the amount of data Google could collect, and thus the greater the value of that data to marketers and advertisers. Google achieved dominance in the search function, and locked in sustainable high profits via the positive network effect.

The same can be said of Facebook: Facebook reaps high profits from its advertising and sale of data collected from users via the positive network effect: the greater the number of users and the more time they spend on Facebook, the greater the value of the advertising and data Facebook sells.

Microsoft established dominance in operating systems and business applications, and has become a kind of utility, skimming profits from continual upgrades of its vast installed software base.

Apple generates artificial scarcity by maintaining its position as the high-status brand of smart phones, laptops and tablets which all offer integrated services. If you want the status and utility of an Apple product, you must pay a hefty premium. As noted in the previous section, the marginal cost of producing another iPhone is relatively modest compared to the price it fetches in the marketplace, so Apple reaps enormous profits on its products.

There is another way to establish a quasi-monopoly: a very high barrier to entry. Microsoft, Google and Amazon have all leveraged their enormous server bases into cloud computing services. It would take tens of millions of dollars to buy the equipment and software needed to compete, and since the dominant companies have other revenue sources, they can afford to cut the prices of their cloud computing services or buy up any new competitor.

None of these highly profitable tech companies earn their billions in profits by manufacturing automation tools. Virtually all of the profitable tech companies generate profits from monopolistic artificial scarcity (Apple and Microsoft), marketing (Facebook and Google selling user data and advertising) or transaction fees (Amazon, Alibaba). (Note that Uber, Lyft and many other highly valued tech giants lose millions or even billions of dollars annually, and their future profitability is highly uncertain.)

Furthermore, each of these very profitable tech companies is unique: there is only one Apple, Google, Facebook and Alibaba. Each is highly profitable due to a monopolistic or dominant position. There can't be ten more Apples, ten more Googles, ten more Facebooks, and so on—there is only room in each sector for one dominant player.

Monopolies and quasi-monopolies (i.e. companies that dominate their sector) are inherently fragile. They attract anti-trust regulatory pressures to break up monopolies, new technologies arise that undermine their dominance, consumer tastes change and commoditized technologies erode artificial scarcities. Assuming that monopolies will generate outsized profits forever is not a view supported by history.

Since we're trying to assess if we're getting richer or poorer, we must ask, do Big Tech monopolies make us richer or poorer?

How Monopolies Make Us Poorer

Monopolies of all types make us poorer in three ways.

First, the profits harvested by monopolies charging higher prices than they could in a competitive market flow to the owners, who are relatively few in number and are concentrated in the top 5% of households. Monopolies thus fuel income and wealth inequality. Since great wealth buys political influence, monopolies also perpetuate anti-democratic asymmetries: the super-wealthy buy political influence to protect their wealth from taxation while the non-wealthy have little political power.

Analyst Simons Chase succinctly summarized the moral debasement of this dynamic: *"What's moral is what's legal and what's legal is for sale."* Moral standards and the rule of law—that everyone is equal before the law—are undermined by concentrations of immense wealth. This debasement of moral standards erodes trust in institutions, which is a key form of societal capital.

To maintain their dominance, monopolies suppress competition and innovation. Big Tech companies famously buy up smaller competitors before they can pose a threat to their monopolistic power.

In these three ways, monopolies impoverish us all.

Taxing Monopolies to Pay for UBI?

On the other hand, can't we tax Big Tech to pay for Universal Basic Income?

It's important to understand the scale of the Big Tech profits in relation to the proposed cost of UBI. The most profitable tech giants—Apple, Google (Alphabet), Facebook, Microsoft and Amazon—together generate roughly $137 billion in annual profits. For context, the gross domestic product of the U.S. is about $21 trillion, and the federal government spends around $4.7 trillion annually.

Proponents of Universal Basic Income (UBI) concede the cost will likely run $1 trillion or more annually. Taxing Big Tech profits at a rate of 75% (a rate that is politically unrealistic) would generate a mere 10% of the annual cost of UBI ($100 billion). A politically realistic tax rate would yield less than 5% of the cost of UBI.

If robotics and AI are intrinsically low-profit commodities, and even the highest-profit tech monopolies generate at best 5% of the cost of UBI, how realistic are claims that *taxing the robots* will pay for trillions of dollars in income distribution to offset the loss of paid work? The answer is such claims are not realistic at all.

The Deflationary Dynamics of Technology

In broad brush, technology—applied science and engineering—has powered industrial-scale mechanization that has turned what was handmade and therefore scarce and costly into manufactured goods available to all at costs that are affordable to almost everyone with an income.

What was scarce became available to all via *commoditization*, the large-scale production of interchangeable components and goods. As goods and services become commoditized, prices decline and the competitive differences between products also diminishes. Despite the many claims of marketers, everything from toothpastes to seats on airlines and thousands of other products and services are interchangeable with negligible loss of functionality.

Commoditization's convergence of functionality has led to the current dominance of marketing as a means of creating the differentiation needed to sell products and services with equivalent functionality.

As a result, digital technology is now integral not only to production but also to marketing. Products, services, labor, conventional capital and marketing are no longer scarce; what's scarce is marketing that penetrates the super-abundance of conventional (and therefore low-value) marketing.

The point here is that commoditization reduces the *value* of what is no longer scarce, as well as the cost. This is why as a general rule, technology is deflationary to prices, employment and profits.

Much media emphasis is placed on the decline in consumer prices generated by technology, as this makes us richer: our money buys more (and better) goods than it did before. The equally significant declines in the value of labor and capital receive much less attention, as lower wages and returns on capital make us poorer.

But here's the thing: despite the many advances in technology of the past 20 years, the costs of big-ticket goods and services are actually *rising*: the cost of college, health care, housing and government services are soaring, not declining. If technology only reduces the costs of a small basket of consumer goods while costs of big-ticket goods and services are rising and wages are stagnating, then we're becoming poorer.

Here are the questions we need answered:

- If household incomes are losing purchasing power due to deflationary trends in employment, does a few hundred dollars in consumer savings annually offset thousands of dollars lost in the purchasing power of income?
- If the quality of commoditized products is declining, then does this offset any decline in price?
- If refrigerators and washing machines that once only needed replacement every 25 years must now be replaced every 10 years, aren't we getting poorer when we calculate the total cost of buying multiple appliances rather than just one?

Let's start by considering the deflationary effects of technology in production, profits and employment.

Deflationary Dynamics: Convergence

One deflationary dynamic is *convergence*, when one new technology replaces an entire host of older technologies.

A classic example is the smart phone, which is now in the hands of billions of people. This single device has replaced an array of once-expensive and profitable products: music players, voice message machines, fax machines, digital cameras, recording devices, video and audio editing tools, scanners, dictionaries, road maps, landline phones, gaming players, books, alarm clocks and so on.

Do the handful of smart phone manufacturers employ more people than all those lost as these industries were made obsolete? It's not an easy calculation to make, but considering that Apple has 132,000 global employees (2019) and 47,000 in the U.S.—a tiny sliver of America's total work force of 160 million—it's difficult to see how obsoleting so many industries and consolidating so many technologies in one device isn't deflationary to overall employment and profits.

While Apple points out that several hundred thousand other jobs have been created by its ecosystem of software and devices, even this number is tiny in the U.S. economy, not to mention the global economy.

Do Apple's annual profits of $59 billion exceed the combined profits of the dozens of industries obsoleted by smart phones?

Consider the deflationary consequences of music migrating from consumers purchasing recordings to paying services for streaming digital files. Royalties earned by creators have plummeted as streaming services take the lion's share of the income, and record labels take much of what's left. An artist who succeeds in getting a million downloads earns a paltry sum—a few thousand dollars, not enough to pay one month's rent for an apartment in cities such as San Francisco.

The False Promise of Profits and Labor in Decline: Uber / Lyft

The stock market currently values the on-demand ride companies, Uber and Lyft, in the tens of billions, based on the expectation that these enterprises will soon reap billions of dollars in profits. But is this expectation realistic?

Consider their business model: these companies *monetize* private vehicles (that is, they don't buy and maintain a fleet of vehicles, they pay owners to use their own vehicles that would have otherwise produced no income) and pay the owner-drivers as "gig economy" free-lancers. This pay is considerably less than the full operating costs of the vehicles and less than conventional wages and benefits for comparable work. The overhead expenses are thus transferred to the drivers, whose net earnings suffer accordingly. Very few of these drivers earn even the median income of full-time government or corporate employees.

Despite the cost advantages of this model, both are losing billions of dollars operating at their current scale. Profits are presumed to emerge when their revenues rise and expenses drop. But given the presence of competition from each other and many other competing forms of transport, how can these services either reduce costs or raise prices enough to turn a profit?

As for eliminating the expense of drivers by investing in self-driving cars: if we look at commoditized business models like Uber and Lyft, we find the labor component is actually rather marginal. Cutting costs by eliminating drivers won't generate profits if competitors also move to self-driving cars and reduce prices accordingly.

This is why projections of immense profits to be reaped by eliminating human labor are unrealistic. Competitors move in lockstep to reduce human labor, and prices decline as each competitor struggles to maintain or increase market share.

Profits only flow to what's scarce, and as noted, the only way to secure scarcity is to establish a monopoly or cartel, i.e. a means to push higher prices on a customer base that has limited or no other options.

While observers tend to focus on traditional taxi companies as the competition to Lyft and Uber, there are many other transport options available to customers, including walking, public transport, biking, arranging a ride with a friend and "black market" ride-sharing that inevitably arises as drivers figure out ways to eliminate Uber and Lyft's share of the fee. Options to get around cities are numerous, and so scarcity is fleeting and contingent.

As for maintaining a competitive advantage by investing in self-driving cars: if we know anything about the push to self-driving cars, we know the competition is fierce and global, and all the necessary parts (sensors, artificial vision software, etc.) are rapidly being commoditized. Self-driving systems will be available to every company in the on-demand ride market.

These services are not inherently profitable. The cost of owning and operating complex and expensive vehicles will never be low, and neither will the liability. Whether the driver is human or a self-driving system, the cost will never be near-zero, and neither will the cost of operating the software and the corporate overhead. Meanwhile, competition cannot be eliminated and so a monopoly that can force higher prices on consumers via artificial scarcity is also not realistic.

As for the impact on jobs: the number of workers who are qualified to be on-demand drivers is large, so there is no scarcity of labor to keep wages high. On-demand companies can increase their share of the fees with little market pushback from the drivers, whose only option to earn more is to drive longer hours, or start competing with the on-demand companies as an informal-economy (black market) service.

Simply put, those earning a living from their creative endeavors and labor are poorer, not wealthier, because commoditization reduces the scarcity value of labor, and convergence obsoletes existing industries. This reality is reflected in the steady decline of labor's share of the US economy from over 65% a decade or so ago to under 60%. That 5% decline might not sound like much, but in a $20 trillion economy, that represents a $1 trillion decline in labor's share. (The chart showing labor's share of national income - a slightly different but similar calculation - can be found on the St. Louis Federal Reserve's FRED database: *Shares of gross domestic income: Compensation of employees, paid: Wage and salary accruals:* W270RE1A156NBEA.)

Convergence and Commoditization Deflates Profits

Convergence and commoditization are as deflationary to profits as they are to labor's share of the economy. As of this writing (mid-2019), the global stagnation of smart phone sales is undeniable, and in response Apple no longer reports iPhone unit sales, lest this reality impact the company's sky-high stock valuation. Not only are sales slowing, but the *upgrade-replacement cycle*, in which consumers opt to buy a new and more costly phone every few years, has stagnated as well, for the reasons explained above: the additional features being offered are no longer compelling reasons to spend hundreds of extra dollars, and existing phones are *good enough* for a decade of use.

As the smart phone industry has been commoditized, prices have collapsed, for reasons explained earlier, and so sales are migrating to the lower price phones (sub-$200), decimating the mid-level phones priced between $200 and $600. The number of consumers globally who are willing and able to pay almost $1,000 for an Apple brand phone is also stagnating.

Apple's strategy to maintain its lofty profit margins is to expand its services in entertainment, but this is a field crowded with well-entrenched competitors, and even success in this low-margin business won't replace the tens of billions of dollars in profit reaped from selling costly smart phones.

If we put these deflationary dynamics of technology together—lengthening replacement cycles, the advance of *good enough*, and the saturation of the market (especially at the high-profit end), we discern a future of declining profits for smart phone manufacturers, especially those at the top tier of the market.

Middlemen No Longer Required (Disintermediation)

In addition to the deflationary effects of convergence, technology also tends to *cut out the middleman*, obsoleting the purpose and value of intermediaries. This process is known as *disintermediation*. One example is banking, which is being obsoleted by micropayment platforms such as China's WeChat, which lowers the transactional costs of consumers' purchases and dramatically reduces banks' credit-card transaction profits. Another good example is travel agencies, which have largely been disintermediated by online travel reservation sites.

Once commoditized, technology becomes cheap enough to spread in novel ways, enabling consumers and enterprises to find ways around highly profitable *artificial scarcity* cartels. Just as peer-to-peer supply chains cut out wholesalers and other middlemen, peer-to-peer lending bypasses the highly profitable *artificial scarcity* banking cartel.

Another example is 3D fabrication technologies, which enable desktop fabrication of a variety of customized parts, a process that disintermediates entire production and supply chains. Costly engineering software is being replaced by free or low-cost libraries, wholesalers of parts are bypassed, and so on.

Declining Quality and Durability

While the conventional view focuses on technology-driven deflation in the price of consumer goods such as TVs, little attention is paid to declining quality and durability, for two reasons: one, these are difficult to measure, and two, they undermine the claim that we're getting richer because prices of TVs are dropping.

This is an example of what I call the *tyranny of price*: since it's visible and easy to measure, price becomes the sole arbiter of value. If the price declines, we're (supposedly) getting richer. But if quality is declining, are we really getting richer, or are we actually getting poorer?

The Limits of Technology

The belief in the ultimate goodness and inevitability of technological advances is often presented as a binary choice: one either believes that technology will eventually solve every human problem, or one is anti-technology and anti-progress.

Suggesting there are limits on technology is thus heretical: for believers, there are no limits.

Let's set aside the false binary choice and ask: are there intrinsic limits to technology, and if so, are we approaching any of these limits?

Technology has a great many intrinsic limits. Technology cannot make what is abundant as valuable as what is scarce. Thus technology cannot make conventional labor—the range of human skills that can be automated or otherwise commoditized—valuable. Nor can technology make conventional capital--now super-abundant due to the issuance of vast sums of low-cost credit by central and private banks—valuable.

The relative abundance of conventional capital and labor is the reason why wages are stagnating globally, and why capital currently earns near-zero yields. Value flows to scarcity, and neither conventional labor nor capital are scarce.

The only forms of labor that are scarce and thus valuable are those types of labor that cannot be cost-effectively commoditized, for example, workers with skillsets that cannot be readily automated.

Technology cannot change the priorities and incentives of those who own it. Technology is only a tool, and people will use the tool to maximize their gain and optimize whatever incentives are embedded in the system. If chopping down irreplaceable tropical hardwood forests is optimized by the incentives to maximize profits, then that's how technology will be applied.

Technology cannot repeal the laws of thermodynamics. Taking a pencil and extending the declining cost of solar panels to zero doesn't negate the physical costs of mining and smelting the ore, shipping the metal to a factory, fabricating the photovoltaic cells, assembling and testing the panels, transporting them to the installation site on vehicles that are expensive to manufacture and maintain, installing the panels, wiring them to inverters and other equipment, testing the system onsite, and returning to perform maintenance and possibly repairs. Since the expected life of the installed panels is 20 to 25 years, the entire expense must be repeated, plus the additional expense of removing and recycling the worn out panels. Therefore the cost of manufacturing, installing, maintaining, repairing and replacing the panels will never be close to zero due to the intrinsic costs in mining, smelting, refining, milling, transporting, assembling, testing, installing, maintaining and repairing the panels.

Even if robots perform all the work, robots are themselves resource- and energy-intensive. Robots are less like a computer chip (with declining marginal costs), and more like a car, an immensely complex and costly assembly of intrinsically resource-intensive components, electronics, computer chips and millions of lines of software coding. Autos cost more than they did a generation ago for all these reasons. As cheap-to-access resources such as metals and minerals are depleted, the remaining ores are more costly to extract; regulations require additional safety features, and extremely complex software is increasingly prone to unanticipated errors.

All of these realities apply to autos, robots and every other complex, resource-intensive machinery.

To become more capable, machines become more complex and therefore more expensive to manufacture, test, maintain and repair. In a very telling edit of reality, those extolling the idea that robots will perform all of humanity's work in the near future overlook these intrinsic costs, and overlook the expensive realities of fixing even simple machines when they fail or break down.

Consider the following two examples:

Example 1. A Japanese auto manufacturer, known for the reliability of their autos, encountered a semi-random flaw that they were unable to diagnose: the accelerator in one model of their cars would become stuck on, pushing the car to high speeds. At first, they attributed the problem to floor mats, then to faulty linkages - and when the problems persisted, to faulty software.

A massive forensic investigation was required to locate the software bugs. This was a major undertaking given that software modules are added to existing coding; manufacturers don't pay programmers to write millions of lines of code from scratch for each new model, due to the high cost. As a result, routine testing did not reveal the fatal flaw. In complex software, intermittent or semi-random errors can go undetected even by extensive testing.

How will robots operating on millions of lines of software coding be any different?

Example 2. Take a relatively simple machine like a clothes dryer. It is basically a metal box containing a heating element and a drum that spins. An electronic board with a digital display operates the machine's cycles and controls. A dryer is thus far less complex than a robot, especially a robot that is capable of navigating the real world.

The dryer control board is relatively simple: a handful of low-cost commodity computer chips and a few circuit boards. Despite the relative simplicity, these boards fail with alarming regularity. This is also true of the electronics in ranges, washing machines and other appliances. The replacement board for the dryer is one-third the cost of a new dryer. Labor adds another third, so replacing the board is two-thirds the cost of a new dryer.

This reliance on cheap commodity electronic components results in the lifespan of modern appliances being measured in years rather than the decades of use formerly expected of purely mechanical appliances.

The ultimate cost of adding features (the functional value of which is often very much in question) is far higher than the sticker price of the new dryer. In the real world, technology has increased costs and consumed more resources for extremely marginal improvements (for example, ten choices of drying cycles rather than five).

Since advocates of robots claim robots will soon do all the work of humanity, consider the vast difference in cost between a robot that operates on a flat factory floor, repetitively attaching one part on a dryer assembly line, versus a robot that arrives onsite in the messy real world and is able to diagnose and repair a broken dryer.

The factory model operates on a flat floor; the repair robot has to navigate an irregular driveway and multiple changes in floor level. It also has to be powerful enough to lift the dryer off the washer (in a stacked configuration), move it to open ground, remove the top, perform the diagnostics, remove the defective board, retrieve the new board, install it correctly, re-assemble the case, test the repaired machine, then lift it back onto the washer.

To repair a dryer onsite, the robot will have to have the strength of a small forklift and a very high level of dexterity and precision motor control. The cost of adding each of these capabilities to a robot is extremely non-trivial, and it won't ever drop to near-zero. Rather, it will only increase in cost even if commodity sensors and chips decline in price. The points of potential failure will proliferate with each new capability and each new level of complexity.

Finally, note that the robot itself is prone to the same kinds of failures that it is designed to repair, but due to its much greater complexity, repairing the repair robot could cost an order of magnitude more than just having a knowledgeable human repair the dryer.

I've performed this exact repair on my own dryer (only a few years old), and other similar repairs on other appliances: a name-brand range that turned on the oven at random times due to a failed low-cost commodity electronic sensor (less than two years old), and an expensive name-brand heavy-duty washing machine, less than a year old, that also failed due to a low-cost electronic sensor.

As I observed before, complex devices are only as reliable and durable as their lowest-quality component. This is as true of robots as it is for any other device.

I happen to be practical, frugal and handy. I've swapped out circuit boards in desktop computers and completed numerous repairs on houses, appliances, autos, etc., and have also learned simple computer markup coding (CSS, for example) as needed. In most cases, I've had to learn how to diagnose and affect the repair on the fly, i.e. without any previous training. As a result, I can make a more realistic assessment of real-world technology's real-world costs than those who have limited experience with fixing complex technology when components fail.

Yet even with me performing the labor, the parts for all these appliance repairs were expensive. Many less-handy people would have paid multiples of this already-high cost just for labor, while others would have bought a new appliance and had the (still-functional other than the one failed component) appliance hauled to the landfill—a perfect example of our wasteful and expensive *Landfill Economy*.

Consider the hundreds of components in a so-called *smart home* designed to save energy and offer more convenience by networking sensors, cameras, appliances, locksets, servers, controllers, Wi-Fi chips and software. The projected advances in security and convenience, many of which are questionable (e.g. just how much value is really added by a refrigerator that can order a quart of milk delivered once it detects a low level in the carton?) come at a very high cost in components, installation, service and repairs, because each of the hundreds of sensors, controllers, Wi-Fi chips are points of potential failure – not to mention the risk of unauthorized remote access. How long will these components last? How long before they must be replaced to function with a new software system? How functional will the system be if even one controller fails?

Given the extraordinary expense of installing and maintain this complex system and the marginal returns in convenience and security, how is this not another system destined for the landfill?

I have yet to find a true believer in *robots will do all the work of humanity* idea who has ever performed even a single repair of a complex system or device caused by a failed board, chip, sensor or software bug - and done so not on a clean factory floor but in the unpredictable real world.

I've also never yet met an avid believer in *robots will do all the work of humanity* idea who has designed, prototyped, tested, manufactured, sold, maintained and repaired robots capable of climbing (or landing) on a roof, diagnosing the cause of a failed solar array, replacing the failed part and cleaning the panels, all for a total system cost that's less than the relatively modest cost of a human repair person.

When Can Something Be Commoditized?

Here is the generalized conclusion: *technology only lowers costs when it commoditizes tasks and products*. When an antibiotic works the same on every patient and can be produced by a variety of companies, it's a commoditized and thus low-cost with predictable outcomes.

Compare a commoditized antibiotic to a complex multi-step treatment that must be custom-formulated to match each patient, a treatment that can only be formulated after multiple tests and analyses on each patient. Since the results are not reliably predictable due to the customization and potential for novel interactions, the patient must be monitored and the dosage/timing of treatments adjusted during the treatment to optimize the results.

This treatment cannot be commoditized like an antibiotic. As a result, it requires more resources, and the cost rises accordingly. Having robots perform much or all of the work won't lower the costs because the robots themselves are intrinsically expensive to design, test, code, maintain, upgrade and repair.

What happens to robots when the cost of diagnosis and repair exceeds the cost of a new robot? The (still functional except for the failed component) robot ends up at the landfill, alongside the dryer with the defective chip, the washer with the failed sensor, the vacuum with a broken plastic part, the car with a defective controller board, and so on.

In the fantasy world of true believers, robots work perfectly essentially forever, until they're replaced by robots that are better and cheaper. Maybe the fantasy extends to using robots to recycle the obsolete and broken robots. In the real world, recycling complex machines is expensive; the components must be separated, and not all parts can be recycled. It may not be possible to cost-effectively re-use or recycle the robots at all, even if the process is automated.

We always end up at the same place: the robots performing the recycling are themselves costly, complex machines that are only as reliable and durable as their lowest-quality component and buggiest module of software. When they fail, they're as expensive to repair as the robots they're recycling.

A system of complex devices that are inherently costly to manufacture and only as functional as the lowest-quality component and software in each is a system optimized for waste and higher costs due to short product cycles/planned obsolescence, i.e. *the Landfill Economy*.

Technology's Purpose: Maximize Profits

It's true that, in service of maximizing profits, technology excels at replacing human labor via mechanization/automation (commoditization of discrete, repeatable tasks and processes). This dynamic also commoditizes labor and capital, as both become interchangeable globally.

If the primary incentive is maximizing profits, technology won't be applied to provide paid work for all or to conserve biodiversity and the planet's resources for the benefit of all. It could be applied to serve these goals, but this would require not just a new set of incentives but a new power structure and new relationships between labor, financial capital, resources, technology and political power.

Technology will not magically conserve our planet's depleting resources and distribute them fairly. In the current socio-economic system, technology is only increasing the momentum of diminishing returns, lower wages, increasing wealth/power asymmetry, more waste and depletion of resources. We must change the incentives, the structure of capital and labor and what's measured, or technology will continue optimizing waste and inequality in service of maximizing financial profits at the expense of everything else.

The Limits of Resources Required by Technology

Those committed to the belief that technology will save us from the current set of perverse incentives and misleading methods of measuring costs and profits turn a blind eye to the resource limitations on technology. Just as solar panels and windmills cannot be nearly free due to the energy required to manufacture, ship, install, maintain, repair and replace them, they cannot be fabricated without the extraction of immense quantities of scarce resources.

Consider the much-touted technologies of artificial Intelligence (AI) such as machine learning. These programs consume enormous quantities of electrical energy, which in places like China is largely generated by burning the dirtiest hydrocarbon source of energy, coal. So much-vaunted A.I. is actually driving the consumption of the most polluting, least efficient source of hydrocarbon energy.

Just as it will never be nearly free to manufacture solar arrays, it will also never be nearly free to manufacture, transport, install, maintain, repair and replace the systems that collect the trickles of diffused energy into densities that are useful or replace the systems that store intermittently generated electricity for later use. While it's pleasant to fantasize about some future technology that might manufacture hundreds of millions of these components out of some abundant mineral, in the world we actually inhabit these technologies use staggering quantities of increasingly scarce metals.

Current battery technology requires lithium, which is not abundant or cheap to mine. Realistic estimates of the quantities of lithium and other essential metals available for extraction with current technologies conclude there aren't enough of these resources to fabricate the hundreds of millions of battery arrays needed to substitute so-called renewable (i.e. *rebuildable*) energy sources for burning hydrocarbons. Like the renewable energy arrays, these hundreds of millions of batteries don't last forever, either; they too are *rebuildables* that must be constantly replaced at great expense.

Every power-storage system requires vast expenditures of capital and resources. Using intermittent solar power to pump water into a reservoir that can then generate electricity as it flows out when needed later will never be nearly free. Pumps are not free to manufacture, transport, maintain or replace; nor are dams, pipelines, turbines, the electrical grid and all the other complex, costly components of this storage system.

Faith that technology will solve every challenge and do so in a way that radically reduces costs is no substitute for engineering realistic lifecycle cost estimates based on what's available and scalable in the coming decades. This faith is nothing but wishful thinking, and as such it is part of the problem, not the solution.

Does Technology Decrease Consumption?

Many people claim that as technology advances, it replaces inefficient technologies with much more efficient substitutes, and this dynamic will lead to a world in which we can have every convenience we now enjoy while using a fraction of the resources and capital we now consume.

Examples of this dynamic include the modern locomotive, which uses far less energy than coal-burning locomotives, and advanced jet engines, which are quieter and more fuel efficient than previous generations.

But a glance at global energy consumption tells us that consumption continues to expand even as various technologies become more efficient. Rather than reduce consumption, efficiencies that reduce costs actually lead to higher consumption.

Recall that every new generation of more efficient devices leads to the wholesale dumping of the obsolete generation in the landfill. Are the efficiencies gained enough to compensate for the immense consumption of resources and energy required to manufacture the new generation? The answer is not straightforward once we start seeking what's been ignored because it's difficult to measure.

Consider air travel and tourism. What was once a low-impact luxury—air travel—has become affordable to billions of people, due in large part to technologies that increased the extraction of oil (which is refined to make jet fuel) and the efficiency of jet engines and airlines. While this vast expansion of air travel has greatly increased the tourist industry, it has also brought millions of tourists into contact with fragile ecosystems, and dumped staggering quantities of the Landfill Economy's stupendous waste in remote locales that lack the resources to gather and dispose of the waste.

Once again, if we limit our calculation to financial transactions, we conclude this unprecedented expansion of air travel has made us collectively much richer. But if we include what hasn't been measured—the environmental toll, loss of biodiversity, the dominance of tourism in local economies, etc.—the gains become questionable.

If we try to quantify what we don't even recognize as a cost, such as the transformation of traditional cultures into purveyors of homogenized luxury tourism, we come to a much more complex calculation of what has been gained and lost. As societies become dependent on the tourist trade for their livelihoods, what happens should tourism slump? What older forms of capital have been lost in the transformation of a once-diverse economy into one that's totally dependent on tourism?

Closer to home, consider the robotic vacuum, which in theory replacing the human labor of pushing a vacuum. The presumption is that this is a labor-saving convenience, but the robotic vacuum only replaces a fraction of the labor required to clean my entire house. As for saving time: since I don't pay myself to clean my own house, there is no reduction in my living costs; there is only an additional consumption of resources and capital. If I pay someone to clean the rest of my house, in many cases the robot didn't do the job very well (the baseboards didn't get vacuumed, etc.) and so the savings in labor is marginal.

Meanwhile, once one component in the robotic vacuum fails, it's dumped in the landfill along with all the other consumer waste, since it's costly to repair—if it can be repaired at all. The vast majority of modern consumer devices are not designed to be repaired – they are designed to be replaced.

Did this supposedly labor-saving device represent an accumulation of capital or a loss of capital? Perhaps we should look for what is presumed not to exist because we can't measure it easily. How about the health benefits of pushing a vacuum around the house? This is good exercise and improves fitness. Given the poor fitness of developed-world citizens and the rising cost of expensive medical treatments for the lifestyle diseases resulting from poor fitness, is replacing one of the few household forms of exercise actually a benefit, for either the owner of the robotic vacuum or society at large? Or is it another reduction in capital that's presumed not to exist because it's not measured?

Taking this one step further, what are people doing with their expanding leisure resulting from labor-saving devices? A great many are increasing their addictive (and therefore harmful) use of smartphones and other screens, an addiction that leads to isolation, loneliness and a variety of psychological disorders. Does this global wave of poor fitness and destructive addiction not exist because we don't quantify it in financial terms? Regardless, it is very real, whether we choose to measure it or not.

If we extend what we know about robot vacuums—that they all end up as industrial waste in a landfill sooner rather than later—to robotics in general, why would the next generation of robots be any different? Why wouldn't they also be designed to be tossed in the landfill once one component in their complex electronics and machinery fails?

Many once-pristine seas and shorelines around the world are now littered with the vast outpouring of an industrial-scale consumerist economy incentivized to maximize profit by reducing production costs and increasing sales. Believers in the magic of technology claim robots will soon be collecting this waste and magically disposing of it in some ecologically sound manner.

But in reality, how much will a robot that can navigate slippery tree roots and soft sand cost? How long will the robot's battery pack last? If drones will be deployed to locate and pick up every empty plastic bottle and every bit of trash, where will the drone take the waste? How many drones will be lost in this ongoing effort? How will the drones get recharged in remote areas? What will be done with the mountains of waste once the robots collect it? Will robots sort the waste? How will it be disposed of? If it can be recycled, how far away is the recycling plant, and how much will it cost to transport the waste to the plant? What will be done with the waste that isn't recyclable?

And lastly: who will pay for the immense costs of this effort? Who will oversee the collection of the drones and robots that broke down in the field? Who will repair them? If you say, robots will repair the robots, then what happens when the lowest-quality component in the repair robot fails, and that robot is also tossed in the landfill?

There is simply no evidence to support claims that technological advances in efficiency reduce consumption or waste. Rather, the constant replacement of hundreds of millions of resource-intensive devices increases consumption and waste. This is a reduction in capital, not an accumulation of capital.

Is Technology Making Us Richer or Poorer?

So is technology really making us richer or poorer? A comprehensive answer requires us to measure the decline in the *value* of goods, services, labor and capital.

Remember: value flows to scarcity, either real or artificially created by monopolies. As technology commoditizes production, obsoletes entire industries via convergence, dismantles intermediaries and bypasses highly profitable monopolies, it destroys the foundations of stable profits.

These dynamics aren't just deflationary to profits and employment; they also erode more difficult-to-measure metrics of quality, durability and *total lifetime costs*—the cost of everything from the mining of the ore and the refining of fuels needed to transport materials to the factory, to the labor and overhead, distribution, debt service, marketing, warehousing, sales, returns, repairs, costs of ownership and disposal.

As commoditization and the concept of *good enough* pressure profit margins, manufacturers resort to sourcing the lowest-cost components - which are usually the lowest-quality components. They also scrimp on testing complex software and systems. As noted earlier, every device is only as functional as every one of its components, and so the failure of even one minor component dooms the entire device to either the landfill or a costly repair.

Shrinkflation, Quality and Quantity

Producers of consumables on the shelves of supermarkets have resorted to *shrinkflation*, reducing the quantity of product while maintaining the fiction of value by maintaining the packaging size. (Regardless of whether the package size declines with the quantity, the price stays the same.)

The quality of goods is also declining as producers attempt to substitute lower-quality ingredients to maintain profit margins. Facing similar pressures on profits, service providers are automating their services and forcing customers to perform work that was once performed by employees (self-checkout, etc.). Any systemic reduction in the quality of goods and services is a form of impoverishment, as wages are no longer able to buy the same quality in terms of durability and reliability.

It's relatively easy to measure the number of jobs in an economy. It's much more difficult to measure the quality of those jobs in terms of financial security and an increase or decrease in the purchasing power of the wages being earned. As I will discuss in a later section, the number of jobs is an incomplete measure of technology's impact on our collective prosperity.

Declining Wages and Essential Big Ticket Items

That labor's share of the economy is in a multi-decade decline is undeniable. (See the St. Louis Federal Reserve's FRED database chart: *Shares of gross domestic income: Compensation of employees, paid: Wage and salary accruals:* W270RE1A156NBEA.) This aligns with measures of inflation-adjusted earned income that show the purchasing power of wages has stagnated for decades for all but the top tier of workers.

Couple this with the fact that there is an enormous gap between the limited basket of goods and services that are getting cheaper (due to technology's deflationary dynamics) and the big-ticket categories (which continue to get more expensive and increasingly unaffordable: housing, government services, higher education and healthcare). Technology may be deflating the price of TVs but it's not deflating the things that cost tens of thousands of dollars annually.

Put these trends together (declining real wages coupled with increasingly expensive big ticket categories), and the only possible conclusion is that wage earners are becoming poorer. The purchasing power of earned incomes is declining significantly, because each hour of labor buys less of the essentials (housing, government services, higher education and healthcare). Items that have declined in price while increasing in quality save a few hundred dollars annually versus thousands of dollars in reduced purchasing power when each hour of labor buys less of the big-ticket essentials.

We began this book with the assumption that technology will make us richer in two ways: (1) it will create more and better jobs while lowering the cost of goods and services, both of which increase the purchasing power of wages, or (2) it will generate profits so enormous and reliable that we can tax these profits to fund Universal Basic Income (UBI), providing incomes to all those who lost their livelihoods to automation.

But what we've found is that commoditization, convergence, disintermediation, innovations that bypass monopolies' artificial scarcities and *good enough* technologies all push profits lower, and the dream of *taxing the robots* to pay for trillion-dollar programs is simply not realistic.

As for technology creating more and better jobs, we've found that the share of the economy going to earned income is in structural decline. The quality and security of jobs is also in decline. As noted in the discussion of on-demand services such as Uber and Lyft, the benefits of monetizing private vehicles flow to the corporations, not the owners of the vehicles, and the earnings from performing these services is lower than regular full-time work. The drivers receive no benefits and their income is contingent on demand and supply; the companies have offloaded most of the risks onto the drivers. Despite the asymmetry of gains in favor of the companies, both Uber and Lyft are losing millions of dollars quarterly, and future profits are far from guaranteed.

As for technology creating more new tech jobs than it destroys: STEM (science, technology, engineering, mathematics) employment has been stagnant for many years, as technology replaces not just low-skill factory work but those working in higher-skills jobs as well. Recall that *enterprises don't have profits, they only have costs*. STEM graduates don't automatically create profits; employing STEM graduates is a cost which may result in profits. If profits aren't forthcoming, the employer goes out of business or closes the program and fires the STEM workers.

Anecdotally, the durability of many goods is in general decline as commoditization pressures profits. If we consider the longer term cost of goods that must be replaced more often, the total cost to the consumer over time is higher than the cost of one initially more expensive but far more durable item. A decline in quality ends up costing us more. This is a largely invisible form of impoverishment.

We asked earlier if robotics and AI could become so profitable that these technologies could be taxed to fund Universal Basic Income for everyone displaced by automation. We found that all available evidence suggests the deflationary dynamics of technology deflate profits, and taxing the few dominant firms reaping significant profits will at best raise a fraction of the costs of UBI.

There is also no comprehensive evidence supporting the claim that technology automatically creates more and better jobs than the ones it destroys. The purchasing power of labor is declining, the exact opposite of what would be happening if technology was generating higher paying jobs on an economy-wide basis.

Clearly, despite the advances of technology, wage earners are poorer, as measured by what is relatively easy to measure (income adjusted for the decline in the purchasing power of wages) and by what is more difficult to measure: the quality and security of jobs, the durability and quality of goods, and shrinkflation.

That many of the technological advances of the 20th century vastly improved human life is obvious. But our focus is on the technologies of the 21st century: the tools of automation, robotics and AI. Our focus in this section is on the potential for these technologies to provide a living income to every worker displaced by automation, and on the often-cited belief that technology inevitably creates more and better jobs than it destroys.

Wishful Thinking

The same dynamics that deflate production costs also deflate profits. There is no evidence to support the claim that deflationary technologies will generate profits on the gigantic scale needed to fund UBI. Labor's share of the economy is in structural decline, while the purchasing power of earned income is diminishing. By any measure, an hour of labor today buys far less than it did at the turn of the 21st century.

These are emotionally unsatisfactory or even distressing conclusions. Humanity's emotional default setting is to cling to whatever promises the least disruption of what we now have and enjoy. This default setting manifests as an unrealistic faith that technology will automatically generate more of everything that's good: more convenience, more comfort, more income, more security, more energy and so on. But this is just wishful thinking.

Certainly the track record of industrialization is indeed remarkable as hundreds of millions of people have been lifted from poverty to new levels of prosperity. But history isn't linear; we can't simply lay a ruler on a trend line and extend it into the future and expect events to follow our linear projection. Emotionally, the possibility that technology won't make life better is unacceptable. Even more unacceptable is the possibility that technology has reached *diminishing returns* with the commoditization of automation: technology will no longer create more and better jobs, nor will it boost profits by the trillions of dollars needed to fund Universal Basic Income and other social programs.

Technology is ultimately a tool, not an ideology or religion. It may be emotionally satisfying to believe in its inherent beneficence, but we are better served by considering it a tool that can be used in a variety of ways.

Technology in service of *eternal economic growth* and profits reaped from a *Landfill Economy* becomes part of the problem, not the solution. If we factor in the systemic erosion of wages and *intangible capital* in the 21st century, technology may not be increasing our wealth at all. Yes, our TVs are getting cheaper (although top-of-the-line TVs still have price tags in the thousands of dollars), and items ordered online are delivered to our doors, but does the value of these improvements offset the losses in purchasing power, quality and capital?

If *eternal economic growth* is unsustainable, and profiting from a *Landfill Economy* is also unsustainable, then we need an entirely new economic model that establishes new relationships between resources, labor, capital, technology and the incentives embedded in our socio-economic-political model.

Section Three: Capital, Labor and Debt

Diminishing Returns on Conventional Capital and Labor

In the second half of the 20th century, capital and labor generated solid returns: savings—*financial capital*—earned a return that exceeded inflation, and as labor productivity rose, so did wages. During the post-World War II era of low inflation, for example, capital deposited in savings and loan institutions earned a mandated 5.25% interest. Costs for housing, healthcare, higher education and taxes were low; even workers with modest wages could afford to rent an apartment and own a used vehicle. A single middle class wage enabled a household to buy a house. Simply put, the purchasing power of wages rose.

But since the beginning of the 21st century, returns on savings and labor have been near-zero – in fact, interest on savings is often negative, i.e. less than the rate of inflation, while wages for the lower 95% of the workforce have stagnated. Measured by what an hour of labor can buy in housing, healthcare, etc., wages have lost purchasing power. So what changed?

This loss of purchasing power is a direct result of Central banks issuing trillions of dollars in new currency (i.e. financial capital), thereby reducing the scarcity value of conventional capital to near-zero. Globally, labor—even highly educated labor—is in oversupply: college graduates are working in cafes because there is little demand for their skills and no scarcity value to university credentials in an increasingly over-credentialed labor force. The only scarcity in labor markets is for workers willing to work for wages so low that they can't support themselves. Employers are unable to offer higher wages because the products and services they produce have little scarcity value in a world with an over-capacity to produce, and so they can't pay higher wages to produce low-value goods and services.

Conventional vs. Unconventional Capital and Labor

While the word *capital* generally refers to money, there are actually many forms of capital: tools and equipment, land, etc.; *human capital*—the knowledge, inventiveness and experience of individuals; *social capital*—the value of social networks and collaboration; *infrastructure capital*, the public roads, utilities, etc. that enable commerce and the free flow of information, and *cultural capital*, the value systems and institutions that enable trust and a shared social contract.

What still has scarcity value in a world of commoditized capital and labor is what we might call *unconventional capital and labor*. Very few individuals are able to come up with a new idea and assemble the means to bring the new idea to the world. This ability to tap *unconventional capital and labor* to come up with new business models and new products and services is inherently scarce.

Steve Jobs and Apple are well-known examples of *unconventional capital and labor* in the tech sector: Jobs famously did not graduate from college, and his university and work experiences were unconventional. The combination of the *human capital* of Steve Jobs and Steve Wozniak and the unique culture of Silicon Valley –a dynamic concentration of intellectual, social and financial capital--enabled the emergence of Apple.

But new ideas aren't limited to technology. The husband-wife team of Douglas and Susie Thompkins, neither of whom had any formal business or design education, started not one but two international brands, North Face and Esprit, with virtually no money or experience. In other words, they had little conventional capital (money or formal training) but were blessed with abundant unconventional capital.

Similarly, the founder(s) of bitcoin (self-identified as Satoshi Nakamoto) published a paper that launched the world's first *Peer-to-Peer Electronic Cash System*, which has expanded into the global blockchain and cryptocurrency fields. These novel ideas spread and gained value without conventional capital.

Unconventional capital and labor are still the exception. The global economy is awash in conventional capital and labor, and so the value of each is diminishing due to the decay of their scarcity value.

Diminishing Returns Due to Commoditization

There is yet another source of diminishing return to consider: the processes of commoditization

To understand why the yield on conventional capital and labor are diminishing, let's consider a high-tech example: a computer chip manufacturing plant. As explained in the previous section, value is a function of scarcity, and once *good enough* products and services are widely available, demand for higher-cost products with slight advantages will be limited, as the advantages simply aren't worth the higher cost to most consumers.

Imagine that a $500 million investment built a chip manufacturing plant that produces chips that double the speed of the previous generation. As noted in the previous section, the profits from this scarce chip slide as competitors enter the market.

Now let's imagine that a $250 million investment could boost chip speeds by 20%. Why can't this upgrade double the speed of the chips? There are physical limits to every technology: availability of scarce minerals, the number of circuits that can be etched on a wafer of silicon, and limits on the rest of the components that work with the chip. If the chip is 20% faster but the components are not 20% faster, that 20% increase won't flow through to the product's output. The chip might be 20% faster, but the computer will not be 20% faster due to the limitations of all the other components. The improvement doesn't impact the end user, and so it has no value in the marketplace. The owner of the plant must make a financial calculation: will the investment boost profits? If not, is there another more promising technology that the $250 million could be invested in? This is known as *opportunity cost*—what opportunities must be passed up to make the chosen investment?

A gamble on a new technology might generate outsized profits if it succeeds, or it might doom the company if it fails. The safer bet is to expand production to increase market share, even if this will reduce the profit-per-chip.

As competitors ramp up production, scarcity value declines. The returns diminish as products are commoditized and incremental improvements no longer tempt consumers to pay more.

In a similar way, additional investments in labor also yield diminishing returns. Training workers on the new machines that boosted chip speed by 100% generated healthy profits, but making the same investment in training for equipment that generates only a 20% gain yields less: the gain isn't significant enough to push prices higher, as the previous generation of chips is still *good enough* for most consumers.

In the larger context and using a different example, spending immense sums for commoditized university educations that don't actually give graduates the skills employers need is a very low yielding investment. Compounding the low return is the over-supply of workers globally with similar college credentials. The scarcity value of a college degree, once substantial when university graduates were a relatively small part of the labor force, has plummeted as the number of college graduates has soared globally.

To summarize: initial investments yield big returns when there is scarcity value for the products and services being generated. But once the products and services have been commoditized, additional investments in equipment and training yield diminishing returns.

Flooding the global economy with more conventional capital and pushing more students through a commoditized education system increases the supply of conventional capital and labor, further reducing their scarcity value. When the yield on conventional capital and labor approaches zero or even dips into negative territory (i.e. negative-yield bonds and college educations that don't raise graduates' incomes enough to pay off their student loans), we're collectively becoming poorer.

Credit, Capital, Labor and Over-Capacity

Technology requires investment, and as a result finance is as much a part of technology as engineering and innovation: technology and finance are in effect one system. The First Industrial Revolution took off not just because new means of production became available; equally necessary was a credit-based financial system that enabled entrepreneurs to borrow capital to invest in new equipment. The new enterprises also needed a workforce and a system for distributing the new goods that were being produced.

This system increased productivity by replacing low-productivity handcrafts with high-productivity machinery. The same capital and hours of labor that earned low returns when items were crafted by hand generated tremendous increases in production when invested in machinery and factory labor.

Labor, credit and returns on investment are interconnected. Investing capital in new equipment increases productivity by reducing the human labor required to produce each unit—the *labor input*.

If capital is scarce and thus costly to borrow, the cost of buying new equipment to further reduce labor costs might not make financial sense. In such a situation, it makes more sense to slowly expand production by reinvesting profits rather than borrow enough capital to replace all the old equipment.

Conversely, if capital is abundant and thus cheap to borrow, it makes sense to borrow money to purchase new equipment that will reduce the labor inputs and thus boost the company's profits. Where the old factory required thousands of workers, the new factory may only need a few hundred workers to produce more (and higher quality) goods.

If capital is cheap to borrow, enterprises have every incentive to reduce their labor inputs by borrowing capital and investing it in automation.

As Marx foresaw, this dynamic leads to *over-capacity*, where every enterprise expands production to grow market share, and as a result the capacity to produce more than the market can absorb also expands. The scarcity value of goods and services diminishes and profits fall.

Global capacity in automobile production, for example, is larger than the market for new autos. Production gluts cause prices and profits to decline. The situation is even more extreme in digital services, which have near-zero costs to produce each new unit (digital song, video clip, etc.)

As historian Immanuel Wallerstein (a leading proponent of *World-Systems*) and others have explained, the cost of labor rises as benefits expand (workers compensation, disability insurance, healthcare, pensions, etc.) and workers' expectations for more financial security increase. The increasing complexity of systems also increases the costs of managing regulation and compliance, a dynamic that raises the cost of doing business and having employees.

As labor costs rise and the costs of capital and automation decline, the incentives favor investing cheap-to-borrow capital in automation to reduce labor inputs and boost production.

If we put all these forces together, it's easy to understand why technology doesn't boost profits or labor inputs, instead it erodes both. With conventional capital and labor abundant and the costs of automation declining due to commoditization, the returns on capital and labor are in structural decline as over-capacity expands. While the costs of goods and services that are being overproduced declines, we're still losing ground as the return on capital and labor drops.

These reduced returns on capital and labor add up to trillions of dollars. But did we save even more trillions on consumer goods and services that fell in price? Given that the major expenses of housing, healthcare, taxes and education are all continuing to rise, the answer is a resounding no.

The Limits of Markets

Markets cannot price in the value of non-monetized natural assets such as diverse ecosystems. Whatever cannot be monetized right now has no market value, as markets lack any price discovery mechanism other than current supply and demand.

There is no way to fix this fatal flaw: markets only price goods and services in the here and now. They lack mechanisms to calculate the lifecycle costs of the goods, degradation of wild fisheries, decline of soil fertility, the opportunity cost of what could have been done with money spent on consumption, and so on. The decline of fresh water aquifers and the shrinkage of glaciers that feed fresh water rivers don't make it into "price discovery" of markets.

If we combine the loss of purchasing power of labor with the tremendous loss of natural capital, it becomes self-evident that adding a zero to financial "wealth" hasn't made us actually wealthier in terms of what we can buy with our labor and what resources are still available to us for future use.

The Limits of Credit-Based Consumption

As noted earlier, technology and finance are really one system. Credit enables the expansion of production, and it also enables the expansion of consumption via consumer credit.

As I have explained in previous books (*Why Our Status Quo Failed, Why Things Are Falling Apart*), there are limits on the expansion of borrowing from the future to fund consumption today. Such a system is only sustainable if future earnings grow faster than the costs of servicing the debt, which rise with every expansion of debt.

As noted previously, labor's share of the economy is in structural decline. This means there is less income to support further expansions of household debt; the limit on expanding consumer debt is already visible.

The political solution to this limit on credit-based consumption is for governments to borrow gargantuan sums annually to fund Universal Basic Income (UBI), which is intended to boost consumption. But as noted earlier, this solution presumes monumental, sustained profits from automation, profits which I have shown will be neither monumental nor sustainable.

Debt that expands faster than income and profits eventually outpaces borrowers' ability to service the debt. This is true for both producers and consumers. There are only two possible outcomes of this mismatch: either borrowers default, collapsing the debt bubble, or governments and central banks create enough currency out of thin air to fund the debt service. This expansion eventually devalues the currency, as the real-world economy isn't producing more goods and services to match the expansion pf the money supply.

In either case, the funding of production and consumption by borrowing from future earnings comes to an end. And if the financial system is no longer able to fund more consumption today by borrowing from the future, both production and consumption will have to be funded out of earnings. As debt-based consumption dries up, the economy spirals into a self-reinforcing contraction, i.e. Depression.

Both technology and consumption are currently dependent on credit that is expanding far faster than the economy, earnings, or profits. Once this unsustainable system breaks down, how will the next generation of devices be funded? How many consumers will be able to afford the new devices and services if they can no longer borrow from the future?

The point here is even if there were no limits on technology (and there are plenty of limits), there still are limits on funding production and consumption with debt that expands faster than earned income and profits.

Markets and Technology Have No Goal

Like natural selection, markets and technology have no pre-destined goals. These constructs have no *teleological destination*; technology isn't going to create full employment for humanity or preserve biodiversity due to some internal structure any more than markets will automatically generate full employment and preserve biodiversity.

We can set desired goals and create incentives that will guide technology and markets to serve those goals, but absent such incentives, technology and markets will respond to whatever incentives are present. The current incentive is to maximize financial profits by any available means. Unfortunately, with this as the guiding incentive, technology and markets are busy destroying biodiversity (to which the markets assign zero value) and employment (since labor is a cost that reduces profits). As a society, we're getting poorer, and this won't change until we systemize new goals and new incentives.

Section Four: Declining Capital in a Traumatized World

If we only look at financial capital measured in dollars, it appears we're getting wealthier – we assume the world is getting more financially secure and that well-being is rising along with financial wealth. However, if we look at all the kinds of capital that are measured in a misleading way or not measured at all, we find global capital is declining (in some cases precipitously); the world is increasingly traumatized by economic insecurity, declines in well-being and losses of natural and intangible capital that no amount of conjured currency can replace.

Cycles of Capital Accumulation and Erosion

Any discussion of capital should be based on recognizing that capital goes through cycles of accumulation and erosion, and cycles of concentration and distribution.

In periods of rising prosperity, capital accumulates across the entire social and economic spectrum: capital invested in transportation infrastructure boosts trade, benefiting a wide swath of the populace; advances in agriculture improves food security, and so on. Conversely, in times of social and economic decline, capital erodes: crop yields decline, trade falters and capital is misallocated in low-productivity activities such as wars, temples and palaces for the ruling elite, etc.

Capital also goes through cycles of concentration and distribution. In the Roman Republic, capital was widely distributed amongst the free male population; a wealthy patrician typically owned ten or twenty times the wealth of a free landowner. In the final stage of the Western Roman Empire, an elite patrician controlled 10,000 times the wealth of a free citizen.

In U.S. history, the Gilded Age of the late 19th century and early 20th century was characterized by increasing concentrations of capital in the hands of a few industrialists and financiers while farmers and laborers had little to no capital. As the 20th century progressed, capital entered a distribution phase, creating a large middle class. In the 21st century, the cycle has reverted back to increasing concentrations of capital in the hands of the elite where a *winner-take-most* dynamic predominates.

These cycles are not just visible in financial capital. They also manifest in other forms of capital that can't be measured in dollars. As social mobility and the social contract fray, insecurity and social discord rise. As environmental destruction increases, the natural capital available to society as a whole decreases.

If we add up all forms of capital, we find financial capital is increasingly concentrated in the hands of the few while the entire society is becoming impoverished as natural and intangible capital declines.

Intangible Capital

There are many forms of *intangible capital*. Some forms can be purchased with money—for example, training which leads to the acquisition of a marketable skill—but many cannot be bought on the market at any price, including health (by which I mean health that is natural and not dependent on costly interventions), social trust, a shared sense of purpose and communities with a collective memory of how to get things done in the real world.

That a great many of the most valuable things in human life cannot be bought like houses or stocks is one of the *ontological limits* of markets: what can't be commoditized can't be bought or sold in the marketplace. Markets are solutions to specific scarcities and surpluses in tangible goods and commoditized services, but there is no market where we can buy social trust or a real-world community.

Consider the proposed solution to automation: Universal Basic Income (UBI), where everyone receives a monthly cash stipend from the government.

How UBI Contributes to Impoverishment

By many measures, communities are in steep decline; many people have little experience of a functional community of social groups, neighborhood friendships, local events, etc. But rather than investing capital in communities, UBI simply transfers money to individuals to spend in the consumerist marketplace: individuals receive money from the central state to spend in a consumerist economy dominated by corporations and cartels with little interest (other than public-relations lip-service) in types of capital that can't be commoditized and packaged: social trust, functional communities, etc. UBI accelerates impoverishment by funneling capital into the corporate-cartel marketplace rather than into forms of shared capital such as functional communities.

Capital Flow Disruptions

How do we measure what's lost in this vast transfer of financial capital into the corporate-cartel marketplace rather than into all the forms of capital that cannot be commoditized? Even if we can't measure it in conventional financial terms, we must recognize the loss of community as a staggering loss of valuable intangible capital, a form of capital that is scarce because it must be nurtured by countless interactions built on trust, purpose and reciprocity, many of which have no price tag.

A key form of capital is *social and economic security*: a secure earned income, a positive social role in one's community, a social safety net, and forms of family wealth that can be passed down to the next generation: family enterprises, the family home and durable forms of money such as precious metals.

Now consider the effect of central bank policies that have stripped the economy of secure returns on savings by lowering interest yields to near-zero (or increasingly, below zero, i.e. *negative interest rates*). This eradication of low-risk, secure returns on capital has forced capital into speculative gambles to earn a positive return. This enormous flood of capital into speculative assets has inflated unprecedented bubbles which have transformed previously low-risk assets such as houses into high-risk casinos where homeowners can lose it all or make a killing depending on their luck or ability to manage the risks of bubbles that inflate and pop with little predictability.

These same capital flows disrupt employment as jobs are offshored to increase corporate profits or capital is invested in automation to eliminate labor costs.

In effect, economic security has declined, because employment is increasingly insecure and once-safe assets have been turned into casino chips. To win in this global high-stakes casino, individuals must either acquire the skills of trading and hedging or they must place their financial security in the hands of managers who may or may not gamble the capital wisely in the global casino.

What price can we place on this systemic loss of economic security? What price do we put on the anxiety and insecurity that now characterize employment and investment in a speculation-driven economy?

Markets and Social Trust

While it's tempting to measure economic security in conventional terms of annual income and assets, this is misleading, for the erosion of economic security is social and psychological, not just financial. The decline in security is a loss of intangible capital.

Even supposedly tangible forms of capital are actually constructs of largely intangible capital. Markets, which are widely presumed to be entirely tangible, are in reality also intangible social and cultural constructs. Markets are not just physical or digital places where buyers and sellers trade goods and services using money as the means of exchange; markets also require *social trust* and mechanisms for redress should a seller cheat customers.

Social trust is a key indicator of wealth and poverty. Nations with very low levels of social trust are poor, while nations with high levels of social trust tend to be wealthy. Like many forms of intangible capital, social trust is a complex, multi-layered construct. It includes trust in strangers and widely accessible structures of trusted third parties which enable two people who don't know each other to trade with confidence.

In poor countries, trust in strangers is low; only family members can be trusted to run the family enterprise. This limits the size of enterprises and encourages nepotism, reducing the potential for expansion. Since there are few if any mechanisms of enforcement or redress, it's risky to trust strangers. The dominant social construct is corruption; authorities are to be avoided since all they do is take your money. Banks and other trusted third parties primarily serve the wealthy.

Conversely, in wealthy countries, social trust is high: there is an abundance of trusted third parties to secure trades, and there are institutionalized mechanisms of enforcement and redress. People and enterprises can trade freely in such markets because the market mechanisms are transparent and trustworthy.

There is no marketplace where we can buy social trust; it is a complex accretion of intangible societal and cultural capital. In the simplified view of conventional economics, markets arise once buyers and sellers gather to trade goods and services, but in reality markets require much more than this to function transparently and fairly. Trustworthy markets are a form of intangible capital, as they depend on societal and cultural capital.

The Effect of Intangibles on New/Small Business Startups/Entrepreneurialism

Starting and operating a small business has long been a key form of *social mobility*: even those without family connections, wealth or formal training can earn a living and establish a positive role in the community by starting a small enterprise. This is not a new idea; prior to the dominance of industrial corporations, self-employment was the norm in many sectors and remains the norm in some economies.

Value flows to what is scarce, and what's scarce and thus valuable is often intangible societal and cultural capital. For example, many have tried to duplicate Silicon Valley's enormous success by building the physical infrastructure and establishing the basic parts of Silicon Valley: research universities, incubators for entrepreneurs, and so on. Most efforts to duplicate Silicon Valley fail to duplicate the results because those seeking to recreate Silicon Valley did not grasp the intangible societal and cultural capital that makes the region so innovative and successful. Such intangibles include: a culture of risk-taking in which failure is expected and valued rather than being a career-ending dead end; a culture that encourages public sharing of information; transparent capital-allocation processes to assess risk and opportunities; high social mobility (i.e. a culture in which social status has much less influence than one's ideas and skills), a high concentration of highly trained workers, and so on.

If we look beyond Silicon Valley, however, we find that it's increasingly difficult to start and operate any type of small business. The costs of rent, insurance, accounting and licensing are rising, as is the complexity of regulatory compliance and the technical requirements to conduct business. It's increasingly difficult to compete against the scale and political power of global corporations. This erosion of entrepreneurism is reflected in the steady decline in new small business formation.

Erosion of entrepreneurial opportunity has many sources. Our educational system is failing to teach the skills required to start and run a small business in today's economy, municipalities increase the burdens on small business, capital that is available to global corporations isn't available to small businesses, and tax incentives are designed to serve large corporations rather than small enterprises. Even intangible capital such as the access to mentors that is necessary to start and run a successful small business is increasingly inaccessible to the average person.

The resulting decline of entrepreneurial opportunities reduces competition, the diversity of local economies and resources available to support local communities— forms of intangible capital that are lost when corporate big-box outlets replace diverse, unique marketplaces (Main Street) that are both competitive and cooperative, as they share and support a community of customers, suppliers and employees.

This loss of intangible community-based capital is painfully obvious when big-box corporate stores open outside town, gutting Main Street small business which can't compete on price. (As noted earlier, these price declines may be more than offset by systemic declines in quality and quantity: the lower price is illusory when quality and quantity are considered.)

Small businesses provide a diversity of jobs, support local producers and contribute money, labor and initiative to local organizations that are the sinew and bones of the community. Conversely, large corporations donate to national organizations, and their volunteer efforts are too sporadic (One-day cleanups, etc.) to sustain local community groups. While it's tempting to measure these volunteer efforts and contributions in financial terms, dollar-based metrics fail to measure what's lost when small business vanishes and the largest employer is a big-box outlet: the caring and effort that goes into sustaining community cannot be replaced with a corporate cash donation. Once there are no community events, no local parades, no dances, no fundraiser breakfasts, no clubs and no place to meet, the community melts into air.

The totality of what's been lost only becomes apparent if the big-box store closes because it wasn't profitable enough. Once the corporate outlets dominate not just retail sales but employment and the sourcing of goods—in effect, a monopoly on jobs, the supply chain and pricing—when the big-box store closes, the local economy has no resources left to replace the jobs that have vanished.

Since the big-box store undermined Main Street and stripped the economy of entrepreneurial experience, few people with the requisite skills and drive to start a business from scratch are left. And since the community dissipated, there is no organization left to raise financial capital or sustain the purpose and effort required to rebuild social capital.

In socially impoverished communities, the big-box store is often one of the few public spaces available to meet friends or enjoy a people-watching stroll. But a big-box store is not a substitute for truly public spaces like town squares and halls, nor is it a replacement for a mix of sidewalk-accessible cafes and other venues to act as a meeting-place for friends. A big-box store is not designed to be a public shared space that serves the community; it exists solely to maximize profits for the owners.

A diverse local economy rich in intangible social and cultural capital is a complex, interconnected ecosystem, in stark contrast to an economy dominated by corporate monopolies and cartels, which are like a monoculture farm that grows one crop. Should the crop be devastated by blight or competition from afar, there's nothing left but bare dirt and weeds.

Adaptability and resilience flow from diversity and the rough-and-tumble of continual experimentation. Corporate monopolies and cartels reduce diversity and limit experimentation in the economy by buying up smaller competitors. The erosion of small enterprises and local community economies in favor of the financial and political dominance of global corporate giants reduces the intangible capital of diversity and the flexibility of self-organizing networks. This reduction in opportunities for self-employment reflects a loss of agency—the ability of individuals to apply their labor and capital to new enterprises—and ultimately a loss of adaptability and resilience.

This lack of diversity harms both labor and capital. Instead of being able to find jobs at a variety of small businesses, workers are limited to the insecure contingencies of the informal gig economy or working for corporate behemoths where those who don't toe the corporate line are sent packing. Capital also has fewer options as small enterprises are risky gambles given the pricing power of global corporations.

When the central government and bank favor corporations over small-scale adaptability, productivity and the economy stagnate, since zombie corporations are never allowed to expire. Capital and labor are frozen in unproductive, inflexible companies, limiting the opportunities for experimentation and adaptable self-organizing networks.

If we add up all these losses in intangible capital, we find communities and individuals are poorer in opportunities, social mobility and economic security. Diversity and adaptability have been pared away by the dominance of centralized financial capital and political power. The modest gains of lower prices (if any, once adjusted for reduced quality) offered by big-box outlets do not replace the vast and varied kinds of intangible capital that have been destroyed or lost.

Intangible Capital: Institutional, Social and Personal

Intangible capital is not limited to any one sphere of human experience. It can be institutional, social or personal.

Trust is a critical form of intangible capital, as are transparency, fairness and reliability. Impoverished countries are characterized by low social trust and institutions that lack transparency, fairness and reliability. Wealthy countries are characterized by high levels of social trust and institutions (public and private) that are operated transparently with high degrees of fairness and reliability.

Access to reliable, accurate information is also an important form of intangible capital, because the more accurate information is available, the better informed participants' decisions will be. Information that has been manipulated to favor insiders or mask real conditions will lead to poorly informed decisions of the sort that erode well-being and financial security.

Flexibility and adaptability are essential forms of intangible capital. Flexibility includes both structural flexibility—the ability to change course as conditions change—and having reserves of capital that can be brought to bear as needed. If a system is so brittle/inflexible that a small decline in revenues brings the system to its knees, the system lacks flexibility and thus resilience (survivability). Which system is more valuable—the one that is resilient enough to weather a rapidly changing environment, or the one that collapses at the first hint of trouble? The answer is obvious.

Networks are inherently more resilient than hierarchies, especially if each node of the network has *agency*, i.e. permission to make decisions without the approval of higher-ups should conditions warrant the fast adaptability of loosely connected nodes. The classic example of this principle is a rigidly hierarchical army in which a single general at the top of the pyramid must approve all actions. This is a *tightly bound network*: each unit is tightly bound to the chain of command which leads up to a single individual. Should that one individual become indisposed, the entire army is frozen and unable to respond.

In contrast, an army that trusts its small-unit commanders to make combat decisions on the fly in coordination with nearby units is a *loosely bound system* capable of responding quickly and effectively to fast-changing combat conditions.

Reserves and redundancy can be tangible—an emergency stash of cash, or a spare emergency radio, for example—but the planning, budgeting and maintenance of *institutionalized* reserves and redundancy is a form of cultural/societal capital. Any organization, be it household, agency or enterprise that has fixed expenses that soak up virtually all its revenue lacks the resources and managerial flexibility needed to adapt to ordinary fluctuations in revenues.

Put another way, organizations that lack *buffers* and the ability to manage them are prone to collapse under the pressure of even modest crises or challenges. History offers many examples of empires that managed crises effectively when they had buffers (grain stored for famines, reserves of labor and money, etc.) and the managerial skills to respond, but then failed when the buffers thinned and the managerial skills—a form of intangible capital—decayed. (The Western Roman Empire is a well-studied example.)

Poor countries are characterized by dysfunctional institutions. Reformers from wealthier countries erroneously assume that the problem is simply a lack of financial capital. While a lack of money might be one issue, there are usually deeper sources of dysfunction, including corruption, rigid hierarchies, tightly bound systems, and a lack of institutional resilience—all forms of societal and cultural capital.

Lack of Accountability

One key intangible form of capital is *accountability*. If authority and responsibility are clearly delineated, then the institutional structure enforces accountability. Transparent incentives and disincentives encourage taking responsibility, and the results are made available to every participant, including those outside the institution.

The dysfunctional institutions in impoverished nations are characterized by a lack of such accountability; no one is responsible and no one suffers the consequences of failure. In such a system, all reforms fail unless accountability is institutionalized and enforced.

In systems lacking accountability, there are no reliable mechanisms for *redress*: if customers are cheated, the formal process is Kafkaesque in its opacity and lack of reliability. In these countries, the only alternative is informal bribes.

Related to accountability, another form of intangible capital is the institutionalized ability to pare back systemic complexity that doesn't serve a core need such as transparency and accountability. Complexity is like a hidden tax on society and the economy, squandering labor and capital that could have been invested productively. Instead, it's churned away in needlessly complicated procedures and glacial bureaucratic processes, all of which can be used by insiders to reduce accountability.

This has a direct bearing on the productivity of the economy and the distribution of capital. When complexity requires special expertise to manage, only the wealthy and insiders can transfer legal ownership of land (as described by economist Hernando De Soto), defend themselves in court, manage complicated financial transactions and so on; everyone else is mired in various forms of poverty due to their labor and capital being limited by their inability to navigate needless complexity.

Accountability and complexity are societal and cultural forms of capital are *scale-invariant*, meaning that they function in a similar manner regardless of the size of the entity: household, enterprise, institution, society. A lack of accountability and unproductive complexity generate failure and impoverishment.

The Current US Economy: Expanding or Contracting?

The overview above has prepared us to survey the U.S. and other developed nations and ask: is the nation's intangible capital expanding or contracting? If we're honest with ourselves, it's obvious that we're losing intangible capital at a precipitous rate.

Trust in institutions is declining rapidly, from the mainstream media to government. These institutions increasingly devote their resources to serving privileged elites and insiders. Trust in the statistics issued by government agencies is declining as the gap between the 3% official inflation rate and real-world cost increases widens. (The Chapwood Index calculated inflation rates of between 8% and 13% annually in American cities, roughly three times the official Consumer Price Index.)

Again, the unavoidable conclusion is that official statistics are being manipulated to serve narratives that protect the privileged few; they're certainly not being issued to serve the interests of the citizenry at large. With basic information being skewed to serve the interests of the few at the expense of the many, a core type of important intangible capital—trustworthy information—is eroding.

Decaying Societal/Cultural Capital

If we review local public and private institutions, we find budgets that have expanded year after year due to higher fixed costs for benefits, pensions and other expenses. Buffers have thinned or are nonexistent, and inflexible, hidebound management is the norm. Local governments are woefully unprepared for the inevitable declines in revenue inherent in recessions, and the typical fix—raising taxes or borrowing more money—will reduce future flexibility and push fixed costs even higher.

We also find public infrastructure is often failing to keep up with population growth. No matter how much taxes and fees go up to pay for improvements, increased traffic congestion, overcrowding, and general decay in public services continues unchecked.

Institutional resilience is decaying as well. Institutions lack the managerial skills needed to navigate rapid change, much less reinvent their outdated structures. The complexity of what were once straightforward procedures (e.g. obtaining a building permit) has soared, as have the non-classroom administrative staffing in education and the non-clinical administration in healthcare. And instead of reducing this vast systemic increase in complexity, technology is increasing it. Rather than improving the core attributes of functional systems—transparency and accountability—we find institutions are increasingly opaque and unaccountable.

The stress created by these dysfunctional systems affects those laboring inside the bureaucracies as well as those seeking redress or compliance with increasingly arcane and costly regulations. Our institutions have lost the ability to discern the difference between complexity that is necessary to sustain transparency versus accountability and complexity that squander scarce labor and capital.

The core output of our institutions is also in doubt. Despite enormous increases in spending on higher education, healthcare and national defense, a variety of studies have found that most college students learn little of practical or marketable value.

The weaponry being produced is so costly and complex the nation cannot afford it—and it may already in fact be obsolete. Indeed, it is apparent that much of the core systems of the nation are obsolete, and the conventional solutions—throw more money and complexity at the problem—are only reducing the nation's capital rather than expanding it. Our well-being is in decline; we're getting poorer, and our dysfunctional responses are accelerating the decline.

This decline in our intangible capital is fueling social anxiety and discord as trust in institutions and the social contract—that each of us have the same rights and opportunities—erodes. This manifests as political disunity: corrosive conflicts between brittle us-or-them camps, the decline in compromise and middle ground, and the failure to recognize the problems may not have traditional political solutions.

There are two additional forms of societal/cultural capital that are decaying: the ability to take off overly optimistic blinders and look squarely at difficult structural problems, and the ability to act effectively once the sources of the problems are understood. While history tends to focus on these forms of intangible capital as manifesting in individual leaders, they also manifest more broadly in societies. Societies that lack these forms of capital tend to be passive and resigned, while societies that manifest these forms of capital tend to be active and dynamic. Societies that lose these capabilities are unable to adapt and respond effectively to rapid change, and so they fail.

Michael Grant described these societal sources of decline in his book *The Fall of the Roman Empire*:

> There was no room at all, in these ways of thinking, for the novel, apocalyptic situation which had now arisen, a situation which needed solutions as radical as itself. (The Status Quo) attitude is a complacent acceptance of things as they are, without a single new idea.
>
> This acceptance was accompanied by greatly excessive optimism about the present and future. Even when the end was only sixty years away, and the Empire was already crumbling fast, Rutilius continued to address the spirit of Rome with the same supreme assurance.
>
> This blind adherence to the ideas of the past ranks high among the principal causes of the downfall of Rome. If you were sufficiently lulled by these traditional fictions, there was no call to take any practical first-aid measures at all.

We see this *excessive optimism* in our current era in the belief that technology will magically solve all our problems - without recognizing the staggering losses in intangible capital or making painful sacrifices to re-order the basic structures of our society and economy.

Clinging to the Old Ways

This brings us to one final form of social/cultural capital: the ability to let go of institutions and ways of doing things that are no longer functional and thus have become impediments to adaptability and resilience. When organizations cling to traditional/conventional structures and procedures regardless of cost, the rising cost of this rigid obedience to failing systems erodes flexibility and productivity, leading to failure and collapse. Once remaining resources have been squandered in a fruitless defense of obsolete systems, there is nothing left to rebuild a new organization on the ruins of the failed one.

The Human Factor: Resistance to Change

As I discussed in my book *The Nearly Free University and the Emerging Economy*, the existing structure of higher education is obsolete, and the cost of maintaining this structure is indebting an entire generation of students. Clear-eyed thinkers such as Peter Drucker understood decades ago that leafy campuses and their unproductive bureaucracies no longer served society and needed to be retired, but our *complacent acceptance of things as they are* won't allow us to adapt.

Impact on Individual Households

So far we've focused on institutional and social forms of intangible capital, but as noted previously, these types of capital are typically scale-invariant, meaning they manifest in individuals and households as well. Households blinded by *excessive optimism, complacent acceptance of things as they are* and *unrealistic assessments* are just as prone to dysfunction and failure as institutions.

Over and above the shared declines in capital, the losses of intangible capital in our individual lives are even more devastatingly obvious than the erosion in societal capital. Workers across the spectrum, from fast-food employees to elite-educated managers in finance, are working harder and longer, yet their economic security and well-being are suffering staggering declines.

Daniel Markovits, author of the recent book *The Meritocracy Trap*, observed: *"A person who extracts income and status from his own human capital places himself, quite literally, at the disposal of others—he uses himself up."*

Markovits also describes the "time famine" experienced by those working long hours, enduring crushing commutes and then bringing work home or going to a gig-economy job. For many parents, time spent with their children has declined to a few minutes a day. How is this not impoverishment?

The number of workers and students suffering from anxiety and depression has reached epidemic proportions. In various polls, half to three-quarters of students report experiencing chronic anxiety or depression. Burnout—the consequence of unending stress—is also soaring, even as the medical community struggles to define the syndrome and come up with better ways to treat it.

Despite spending almost 20% of our Gross Domestic Product (GDP) on healthcare, our psychological and physical health is declining if we consider the systemic increase of chronic diseases (metabolic disorders, etc.), poor fitness, self-medication, addiction and a host of mental health issues. How is this not a decline in well-being?

While an endless parade of tech-sector pundits promote the idea that technology—the Internet of Things (IOT), 24/7 connectivity, etc.—are making our lives easier, everyday life suggests the exact opposite: technology is increasing the complexity and time pressure in our lives, not decreasing it.

A startling number of those spending hours per day on social media report feeling depressed and lonely; indeed, a sobering number of digitally connected youth report having no real friends. How is this not a tragic decline in social capital?

I've discussed the causes of our *winner-take-most economy* in previous books: the decline in yields from ordinary labor and capital, the global commoditization of capital and both low-skill and specialized labor, and financialization that has skewed returns to favor the already-wealthy and those with the skills to navigate fast-changing, speculative markets.

The *winner-take-most economy* has produced sustained losses of financial and intangible capital for the majority of participants. Adjusted for real-world inflation, the wages for the bottom 95% of workers have stagnated at best, while the higher returns on speculative capital have favored those who own the kinds of capital that have soared in value.

The decline in intangible capital is equally striking. Social mobility has plummeted by many measures: the number of people who earn more than their parents has declined sharply in just a single generation, and the advanced degrees issued by elite universities—the tickets that must be purchased to win the feverish competition for plum jobs—go mostly to the offspring of wealthy families who have the means to send their children to elite prep schools, hire tutors, etc.

The *winner-take-most economy* has marooned many people in dead-end jobs that everyone knows are inessential, what author David Graeber calls *BS Jobs.* Not only do these jobs not pay enough to support a middle-class life, the opportunities for advancement are limited and the superficiality of the work robs the workers of purpose and a positive social role.

Social mobility is even lower for those excluded from the workforce due to a felony conviction or a lack of skills and social capital. Depending on social welfare or cash-only work in the informal economy, these marginalized members of the workforce have few positive social roles to bolster their self-respect or serve as role models and few ways to contribute to society.

Even when gainfully employed, workers are increasingly alienated from the winner-take-most economy due to burnout (overwork and stress that triggers a collapse of their ability to function), a mismatch between their skills and the demands of employers, the burdens of student loans, the struggle to change careers in mid-life due to layoffs and obsoleted skills, and a general sense of having failed the intense competition to "win" in a globalized, commoditized, financialized economy.

Rather than feeling financially secure, we feel insecure. Rather than feeling we have a valued, purposeful role in our community and society at large, we feel undervalued and marginalized. Rather than being confident that we'll be better off than our parents, we sense that their lifestyle is out of reach. How are we not poorer from all these declines in intangible capital? How is this erosion of capital not traumatizing?

Authenticity and Trust

Digging deeper into the types of intangible capital we don't even recognize (much less attempt to measure), we find that yet another important but poorly understood form of capital, *authenticity*, has declined. Authenticity is not limited to individuals; it also has social and economic facets.

The modern economy places a premium on maintaining a public self that is positive, follows directives, is willing to learn, etc.—all the traits that are desirable in employees and the self-employed. We all understand that this public self might not authentically reflect our private selves. For example, we might be introverted by nature but maintain a superficially outgoing personality at work out of necessity.

This dual self, public and private, is not necessarily inauthentic. But the pressure to succeed in a *winner-take-most economy* has pushed some people into falsifying their accomplishments, hiring others to write their academic thesis, claiming others' work as their own, and so on—a severe devaluation of authenticity with financial, social and psychological consequences.

The decline of social mobility and opportunities for positive social roles in the real world has left many people groping for some way to feel good about themselves, and social media offers them an alternative universe in which to exaggerate and glorify themselves, a narcissistic exploration of the far reaches of inauthenticity.

Democracy has lost authenticity as our system of governance has transmogrified into a *pay-to-play* scheme that protects insiders at the expense of everyone else: the faces change but the structures and policies remain the same.

The financial system is equally inauthentic, as central and private banks create money out of thin air by borrowing it into existence, an expansion of *claims on real-world resources* that is entirely disconnected from the actual expansion or contraction of real world resources.

As noted in the previous section, trust is a key form of intangible capital in all realms: personal, economic, social and political. The ruling elites no longer allow the people to make decisions, since they might conflict with the elites' rigging of the political and financial systems to their own benefit. As a result, the non-elites no longer trust the state—which, in our *pay-to-play* union of wealth and power, serves the interests of the few while claiming to serve the many. Nor do they trust the corporate media, which touts the status quo and ridicules dissent. (Recall that the vast majority of sectors are dominated by a handful of corporations: six media companies own the vast majority of media outlets, a handful of defense contractors control Pentagon contracts, a handful of hospital chains, pharmaceutical companies and insurers control healthcare, and so on.)

Efforts by the elites to simulate trust are inauthentic, and only serve to reveal the catastrophic loss of trust in institutions, technocrat experts and the financial and political systems.

Life itself loses its authenticity when everyday living is stripped down to an endless loop of work, commute, 24/7 connectedness, a mad rush to plow through chores and then a homogenized pastime of consumption. We've reached the point of suicidal blindness: since authenticity can't be easily measured, it really doesn't exist.

When the built environment becomes corporatized, it loses its authenticity as homogenized ersatz versions of what was once authentic become the norm. Resorts the world over look and feel more or less the same, simulations of what was once unique to a specific place and culture. Here's an example: during my first visit to China in 2000, we witnessed old neighborhoods of plastered bricks and tile roofs being bulldozed, and the new buildings that replaced them sporting shiny fake tile roofs, a crass mimicry of the authentic architecture that had been destroyed. Now the few remaining traditional houses (*hutongs*) are scarce and very expensive, as elites have come to value what little authenticity remains.

As corporate chains homogenize the world, places lose their soul. Whatever's still unique is stripped of authenticity by marketing: Old Town becomes just another tourist trap. What has been lost as maximizing profit via homogenization and marketing strip away authenticity? Life is poorer.

How is authenticity not a vital form of intangible capital?

This overview of intangible capital cannot possibly do justice to such a profound, nuanced topic, but hopefully it's enough for us to understand that just because intangible capital can't be easily measured, that doesn't mean it doesn't exist. Not only does it exist on multiple levels, it's as important to our understanding capital and well-being as tangible capital.

How is this systemic erosion of intangible capital not traumatizing?

Negative Network Effects

I am indebted to analyst Simons Chase for his insightful concept of *negative network effects*. The *network effect* describes the value added to a product or service by each additional user. Put another way, the more people start using a service, the more valuable that service becomes to every user. Prime examples include the telephone, the Internet, and social media sites. When the Internet was limited to a small number of sites and users, its value to users was also limited. Now that billions of individuals and almost two billion sites are online, the value to each user—and to the economy and society—are much greater.

New users are only seeking to add value to their own lives, but by joining the network, they add value to every user and the network. As the network adds participants, it become more attractive to new users, and this increase in network value generates a positive feedback loop.

The Network Effect is expressed mathematically in *Metcalfe's Law: the value of a communications network is proportional to the square of the number of connected devices/users of the system*.

As I understand Mr. Chase's concept, a *negative network effect* results when the addition of additional users ultimately decreases the capital of users and society. What causes the decline in value as more users join the network? Once the majority of users join the network, it can be *captured and exploited* by corporations or governments. In the case of social media, what began as a social network becomes a market dominated by the corporation that operates the platform.

For example, once the majority of the populace has joined a healthcare system, then corporations that capture that market (via lobbying, regulatory capture, marketing, etc.) can raise the prices of their medications without regard for the social and financial costs to the members or society at large. In effect, once a network becomes dominant, competition ceases and the network is ripe for exploitation that reduces the quality and raises the costs for every member and for the society at large. Here is Mr. Chase's explanation:

> *W. Brian Arthur, the economist credited with first developing the theory, described the condition of increasing returns as a game of strategic positioning and building up a user base to the point where "lock in" of dominant players occurs. Companies able to tap network effects have been rewarded with huge valuations and highly defensible businesses.*

But what about negative network effects? What if the same dynamic applies to the U.S.'s pay-to-play political industry where the government promotes or approves of something through a policy, subsidy or financial guarantee due to private sector influence? Benefits accrue only to the purchaser of the network effects, and consumers, induced by the false signal of large network size, ultimately suffer from asymmetric risk and experience what I'm calling a loss of intangible net worth for each additional member after the "bandwagon" wears off.

This is the essence of privatizing profits and socializing losses, at a national scale. Massive numbers of people blithely buy: houses that turn into lottery tickets, legal drugs that are highly addictive, food that has been processed into junk, and an education that is nothing more than a financial debt. When the giddy illusion of renewal wares off, unsuspecting consumers are left with massive debts and/or shortened diseased life.

In the case of strong negative network effects, the creators' knowledge of product and/or policy's designed-to-fail nature obviates the need to bribe the government to get scale with distribution. The information asymmetry of the creator/purchaser of negative network effects is exploited by government approval because people assume the government's approval implies beneficial outcomes. The executives of for-profit colleges knew the degrees were worthless: so they cash out of IPO stock before corporate bankruptcy, politicians collect millions in contributions and post-retirement consulting, and student are left stuck with a worthless degree and massive government-backed debts that cannot be discharged.

Once the owner of a network locks in dominance, the network serves the interests of the owner at the expense of the users and society at large. Higher education is good example in the U.S.: since a college diploma is viewed as a must-have ticket to a middle-class life, universities and colleges have locked in their dominance via their monopoly on accreditation, and they can raise the cost of their diplomas without regard to the declining value of the diploma to users (students) or society at large. (Search the web for the report *Academically Adrift*.) Each additional student reinforces the cartel's dominance and enriches higher education insiders and lenders at the expense of all students and society.

Facebook and similar companies manifest *negative network effects* as they extract billions of dollars in profits by marketing users' data and exploiting users' weaknesses to strengthen their "engagement" (stated less abstractly, their addiction to social media) to collect more data to sell. The full social cost of these *negative network effects* are difficult to tally, but studies have found that loneliness and alienation are correlated to how many hours a day individuals spend on social media. (An Internet search brings up dozens of reports such as NPR's *Feeling Lonely? Too Much Time On Social Media May Be Why*.)

Negative network effects typify our economy and society. How can the resulting decline in individual and societal capital not be a form of all-too-real impoverishment?

The Decline of Irreplaceable Natural Capital

That Earth's resources are not infinite is obvious, but the reigning narrative of eternal growth demands that we believe technology will advance so we can continue to extract ever-larger quantities or replace depleted resources with new materials. Thus the corporate media continually touts an endless extravagance of laboratory discoveries that promise to make food, energy and water—what I term the FEW resources—inexhaustible. But these promises of miracles soon disappear once they encounter the real world of costs and scale. Very few of these promising technologies scale up to levels that would make a difference, and even fewer pencil out financially: they consume more resources and capital than they produce.

All the current discussion of climate change—how much of it is human-caused, how it can be fixed by carbon credits that trade just like all the other speculative financial instruments that so enrich the elites—serve to distract us from the suicidal insanity of the eternal growth model and the absurdity of the magical belief that we can always extract more to consume and do so painlessly thanks to technology.

The contradiction is obvious: rather than consume less, the plan is to consume more but use technology to magically reduce the consequences and the costs of ever-expanding consumption.

While we entertain fantastically costly technological schemes for sequestering carbon, the real world is traumatized by irreplaceable declines in natural capital and catastrophic reductions in natural buffers. While in developed nations, it's possible to breathe the clean air and enjoy the pristine forests of wilderness parks and chart the progress being made in reducing urban air pollution, and come away with the belief that environmental values and regulations are restoring natural capital. This is an inaccurate, incomplete picture, and is simply the result of wealth protecting its homeland. Yes, some natural capital is being restored in the planet's wealthy enclaves, but hidden out of sight beneath the ground, irreplaceable aquifers are still being drained and the affordable-to-extract deposits of oil and gas are being depleted.

Once you leave these wealthy enclaves and enter the world the wealthy are exploiting to fuel their insatiable consumption, we find a much different picture: forests burning, glaciers that feed rivers melting away, water shortages affecting hundreds of millions of people, depleting reserves of oil, gas, lithium and other minerals, vast seas stripped of wildlife, and insects dying in untold billions, including the insects humanity needs to pollinate its own food sources. (A recent headline that splashed across the Internet is an example: *Half A Billion Bees Drop Dead In Brazil Amid Jump In Pesticide Use.*)

The fantasy that technology can enable a painless eternal expansion of consumption is wedded to the equally absurd fantasy that we can pay for any amount of techno-wizardry we desire by simply creating more money by borrowing it into existence. As noted previously, this financial wizardry assumes that simply *creating more claims on dwindling natural capital* will magically extract more natural capital to fuel our eternally expanding consumption.

This is an intrinsically faulty assumption, for the only capital that can be invested is *surplus capital*, and adding zeroes to our money supply doesn't increase either surplus capital or natural capital.

Human settlements grew from rude scattered villages into cities only when agricultural surpluses created surpluses of labor that could be devoted to building cities and performing the labor required to sustain an urban lifestyle: specialized labor, a managerial class, markets that enabled an expansion of trade, etc. Civilizations that generated surpluses had the capital to build cities and temples. When the surpluses dried up (due to drought, plague, wars, etc.), temple building stopped, as there was no longer a surplus of food to feed construction crews and a managerial elite.

Adding zeroes to our money supply creates the illusion that we can create surplus capital out of thin air. But we only create surplus capital by consuming less than we produce, and it's highly doubtful that we're producing any real surplus after we subtract financial legerdemain and the costs of servicing all the debt we created when we borrowed the money into existence. (Recall that money is created by issuing debt: a government bond, a home mortgage, etc.)

The asymmetry between the extraordinary expansion of our money supply and the decline in real-world natural capital will eventually shatter the financial system, since creating 10 more claims on a single unit of oil, lithium, fresh water, phosphate, etc. doesn't magically create 10 more units of oil, lithium, fresh water, phosphate, etc. or magically increase surplus capital ten-fold.

Here is a simple example of this dynamic: it costs X amount of energy, materials and labor to extract, refine and transport a barrel of oil. After the cheap-to-extract oil is depleted, it will now cost 2X to extract, refine and transport a barrel of oil. The more capital that's required to extract, refine and ship a barrel of oil, the less capital that's available for other investment or consumption.

While technology (fracking, etc.) can lower the costs of extracting oil, every technology requires capital, resources and labor. Every technology has physical or cost limits. In the case of fracking (i.e. *tight oil*), the limit is the depletion rate of each well: 18 months or less. That means thousands of new wells have to be drilled every year to maintain production, and thousands of depleted wells capped.

The point here is the technology required to extract and transport resources such as oil and all the scarce minerals required by so-called renewable alternatives (lithium, rare earth metals, etc.) lowers costs by reducing labor, and labor is only a limited percentage of the total cost. Even if extraction, processing and transport is all automated, this doesn't mean the resources become any cheaper to extract. Digging enormous holes in the earth with gigantic excavation machinery, all to refine a relative handful of scarce minerals, will only become increasingly expensive as the cheaper-to-extract resources are depleted. Subsequent wells must be deeper, the pit-mines larger, the distances traveled to market farther, and so on.

Most importantly, no technology can replace glaciers once they've melted away, fisheries that have been wiped out, or soil that's blown away. While the regenerative power of Nature is often promoted as the solution to environmental damage, this power is not guaranteed: fragile tropical soils turn to hardpan once the forests have been clearcut and a few crop harvests have depleted the nutrients, and fisheries that have been wiped out don't magically regenerate.

Similarly, another illusion we hold dear is that there will always be another resource we can substitute for a depleted resource: we can substitute solar panels for oil, fish farms for wild fisheries and so on. But many of the resources being depleted are irreplaceable; there is no substitute for aquifers, glaciers, fertile soil, bees and so on. Once these resources are depleted, there is no substitute, no magical technological solution and no magical monetary solution. As resources are depleted, the world is becoming poorer, and wishing it wasn't so doesn't make it so.

Money is a social construct, an artifice of human culture. It is not equivalent to natural capital. We assume that money will always buy real-world food, water and energy. But as a social construct, money can disconnect from the real world. Once money can no longer be exchanged for natural capital, it is worthless. Put simply, adding a zero to our money doesn't mean we can magically buy ten times more real-world resources. We can manipulate money because it's a social construct, but we can't exert the same magical power over the real world of natural capital.

Section Five: The Structure of Power

Our System of Elite Dominance: Inputs, Processes, Outputs

Why is our socio-political-economic system (the status quo) so resistant to changing what we measure and how we measure it? Why does this global system go to such extraordinary lengths to support the idea that financial measurements of wealth are accurate rather than terribly misleading?

The answer is the same old story: elites resist whatever threatens their power and privileges. The elite ideal is a self-perpetuating system that maintains their power and privileges as its core function. In the language of systems, *the only possible output of this system is the perpetuation of elites' power and privileges.*

This system rests on the following basic intellectual foundations:

1. One is that *the system is open to all, and elites have risen to the top via merit*. Thus any failings are individual, rather than systemic.
2. The second one is *the system measures what's important and optimizes it to the benefit of all*. What's most important is financial profit, and so the system optimizes profits. The core narrative is that *this is the only possible system that is fair and beneficial to all*, and so not only it is worthy of our support, it is a manifestation of human nature: there are no alternative ways of organizing human life that are equally incentivized in ways that benefit everyone.
3. The third foundation is *growth is the only path to prosperity*. Capital and consumption must continually expand or the global economy will slide into the misery of depression.
4. The fourth is *technology benefits us all*. Any technological advance is, by definition, assumed to be beneficial to everyone, and the faster advances spread throughout the global economy, the broader the benefits.

These foundational ideas are promoted so effectively that they are rarely even identified *as belief structures rather than facts*. The status quo has a complete arsenal of techniques to marginalize, ridicule and dismiss dissenters.

Understood in this manner, it's clear that this intellectual construct is the perfect defense of *a system rigged to benefit the few at the expense of the many*. Any criticism is sour grapes from those who didn't merit elite status, and anyone questioning growth and technology is harming everyone. In this system, measuring financial profit and wealth is as natural to us as measuring the weather.

Power and privilege arise not just from intellectual constructs but also from political, social and economic structures. To understand the structure of power, we need to understand how systems work.

Natural and human systems are inherently complex, but beneath this complexity all systems share one basic structure: *every system has inputs and processes, which yield outputs*. Change the inputs and/or processes and the outputs will change. Leave the inputs and processes unchanged, and the outputs will remain unchanged.

As systems analyst Donella Meadows explained in her seminal paper *Leverage Points: Places to Intervene in a System*, new feedback loops are leverage points. Adding a new source of information, for example, by *measuring something that had previously not been measured*, changes the inputs and thus the outputs of the system.

An example of information feedback cited by Meadows is increasing the visibility of household electricity consumption: when the meter is in the entry hallway instead of the basement, the residents cut their electricity use by 30%. In this case, what was added wasn't a new measurement; what was added was easy access to the information that was already being displayed.

This raises the question: what if well-being, external costs and intangible capital were measured and posted publicly, rather than the stock market being presented as the primary metric of prosperity? How would seeing our intangible wealth decline even as the stock market moved higher affect our decisions?

We can imagine how quickly the elites would move to suppress this new feedback loop. Meadows described the resistance to adding information that could undermine elites' privileges and power:

> *"There is a systematic tendency on the part of human beings to avoid accountability for their own decisions. That's why there are so many missing feedback loops—and why this kind of leverage point is so often popular with the masses, unpopular with the powers that be, and effective, if you can get the powers that be to permit it to happen (or go around them and make it happen anyway)."*

As Meadows observed, *"Power over the rules is real power."* Control of the rules-making processes (governance) and the manufacture of narratives (mass media) enables elites to maintain their privileges and power. This control limits public information and dissenting narratives by suppressing or marginalizing any feedback loops and narratives that threaten elites' power.

Control of the rules also enables elites to amass information flows that are confidential—either privately owned (Google, Facebook, et al.) or state-controlled—that are accessible only by elites, who sell this information (search results, purchases, social media engagement, facial recognition, etc.) for vast profits. Governments use this trove of information to identify and track any citizens who are deemed threats or potential threats.

Where less self-serving citizens might consider these secret flows of information a violation of privacy and civil liberties, elites have the power to legalize and normalize whatever serves their interests.

Recalling the excerpt from Daniel Yankelovich that opened our inquiry, *what the current system can't (or won't) measure doesn't exist.* Every autocracy craves the power to deny the existence of whatever might threaten the elite's control, as there is no need to debate, suppress, criminalize or marginalize what doesn't exist.

The Internet once offered the public an avenue to, in Meadows' phrase, *go around them and make it happen anyway,* but the Web is quickly being limited or brought under the opaque control of autocratic private wealth and state agencies.

Returning to the basic structure of systems, if the inputs are limited, and the processes are tightly controlled, then outputs are also controlled. Once the inputs and processes are locked, *there is no other possible output of the system.* Reform is a cruel charade if it doesn't change the inputs or processes.

A system is a machine with an internal logic defined by the inputs it accepts and the processes it executes. This internal logic may sometimes generate contradictions that the machine is incapable of resolving.

For example, the system may be highly destructive in its final end result (output), but if its internal reward structures (i.e. incentives) are fulfilled, it will continue its path of destruction. This is much like cancer grows due to its internal logic: the cancer cells are programmed to reproduce and compete for resources, and the resulting death of their host—a demise that triggers their own death—is not an input in their internal logic. Cancer cells don't measure the damage being done to their host, or calculate the consequences of that damage, including the eventual death of the cancer cells themselves. In the system of the cancer cells, *the fatal damage to the host is not measured and thus it doesn't exist.*

Yet the damage is real, and so the cancer cells outcompete the healthy cells and kill the host. In the moment of their own death, the only input the cancer cells are programmed to accept is that the resources needed to reproduce are no longer present. Their demise is a direct result of their competitive success.

Cancer cells are blindly self-perpetuating, and our socio-political-economic system is much the same: its internal logic perpetuates elites' power and wealth even as the internal contradictions of the system generate its eventual destruction.

Self-perpetuating systems accept inputs that measure the success of self-perpetuation and ignore the costs. A timely example is the high percentage of students attending elite universities who are the children the elites. Despite the public-relations veneer of meritocracy, the wealthy and powerful have the means to game the system: alumni are still granted undisclosed privileges, ghost writers can be paid to write essays, tutors can boost the SAT scores of elite offspring, and all the extracurricular activities elite universities measure can be arranged. The costs to society of this self-perpetuating system are not recognized, much less measured. The systemic loss of integrity and public faith, the systemic loss to society and the economy by advancing elite mediocrity rather than the truly gifted, and so on.

Political power is another example of a self-perpetuating system that ignores social costs. The wealthy buy political influence, which protects them from the negative consequences of their actions. Thus the manufacturers of addictive opioid drugs bought political protection from the consequences of their misleading claims that the drugs were safe and non-addictive. Hundreds of thousands of patients who were prescribed the drugs have died while the manufacturers collected tens of billions of dollars in profits. Now that the systemic costs of this profit-maximizing scheme are undeniable, wrist-slap penalties are being distributed by government regulatory agencies.

The entire maximizing-profits machine only accounts for profits, costs of production and return on capital. External costs such as environmental damage are ignored; once again, *if these costs don't get measured, it is assumed they don't exist*. So the Texas-sized gyre of plastic waste in the Pacific Ocean isn't recognized as a cost of the profitable production of plastic, much less measured. It exists in the real world, but not in our accounting.

If all the external costs were measured and accounted for, the production of plastic would no longer be profitable.

This is one of the *ontological contradictions* (internal contradictions that arise from the very nature of the system) at the heart of our socio-political-economic system: just because the system doesn't recognize or measure costs (i.e. accept these costs as inputs) it doesn't mean these costs don't exist. Like cancer, our system doesn't accept as inputs the consequences of the self-perpetuating profit-maximizing machine. Like cancer, which accepts its own expansion as the sole measure of success, our system only recognizes profits and the expansion of financial capital as success.

That this purposefully blind measure of success will destroy the entire system goes unrecognized and unmeasured. Since we don't measure external costs, we assume they don't exist. Yet they *do* exist, and their long-term costs are undermining the system. We don't accept this *ontological contradiction*, so assume it also doesn't exist.

If we step outside the internal logic of cancer cells and our status quo, we see that the world is becoming poorer in every meaningful way even as the cancerous system declares all is well because profits are rising.

Systems whose goal is maintaining the same output regardless of cost—in our system, the desired output is elite control of the economy and society—must discount or ignore information flows and inputs to achieve the desired output. But these distortions destabilize the entire system, since restricting information and ignoring the real inputs and actual outputs strips the system of feedback that is essential to maintaining stability.

In manipulating information, inputs and processes so the system maintains their privileges and power, the elites have destabilized financial capital, and laid waste to the intangible capital that underpins civilization. This is the second *ontological contradiction* eating away the heart of our system: by fixing the output (by ignoring the actual output)—that the system must continue to function so elite control is maintained—the essential feedback of real-world information is stripped away, leaving the system increasingly detached from reality and prone to catastrophic self-reinforcing instability. (The 2008-09 Global Financial Meltdown was a limited example of this dynamic.)

Limiting information flows can modify perceptions but it can't modify the real-world output of external costs. Elites can convince themselves that they're getting richer and sell the lower classes the happy story that we're all getting richer, but this manufactured narrative doesn't change the reality that we're all getting much poorer—even the elites clinging so desperately to their privileges and power are getting poorer.

Donella Meadows aptly summarizes how systems designed to measure only what's convenient to measure impoverish us all:

> *"No one can define or measure justice, democracy, security, freedom, truth, or love. No one can define or measure any value. But if no one speaks up for them, if systems aren't designed to produce them, if we don't speak about them and point toward their presence or absence, they will cease to exist."*

Given our system's incentives to optimize profit and measure only financial gains and losses, the only possible output is the destruction of natural and intangible capital. Since what we don't measure is treated as if it doesn't exist, the only possible output of this system is the destruction of the entire system.

This is akin to cancer killing its host and ultimately itself; up to the moment of the host's demise, the cancer is "winning" the competition for resources, just as elites are winning the competition for resources, income and wealth.

The Power of Platforms: Ownership of A.I. and Information Flows

To maintain their dominance, elites must control the most profitable and powerful economic tools. In the late 19th and early 20th centuries, the most profitable economic tools were quasi-monopolized industrial production and banking. In today's economy, a handful of financial giants continue to generate outsized profits and influence, but industrial production has been eclipsed by quasi-monopolistic platforms that use proprietary software and artificial intelligence (AI) to optimize the distribution and marketing of goods, services and information flows. By *quasi-monopolistic* I mean entities that exist in theoretically competitive markets but have the scale, proprietary tools and market power to dominate their sector as well as the political power to maintain their dominance via *regulatory thickets* that stymie smaller competitors.

Since production has been commoditized, profits generated by manufacturing components and assembling goods have fallen to near-zero. This is why production was allowed to shift to Asia; it wasn't profitable enough to keep in the US.

Outsized Profits from Data Collection

Today's great wealth-creating enterprises—Wal-Mart, Amazon, Apple, Facebook, Google, Alibaba—are quasi-monopolistic platforms that either distribute globally sourced goods and services (Wal-Mart, Amazon, Alibaba), add value to commoditized products via proprietary software and brand loyalty (Apple), or collect vast streams of data from users that can be sold for immense profits to marketers (Google and Facebook). In fact, all of these dominant corporations collect massive amounts of data from users and customers, and then extract value from these data hoards.

The corporations own the data collection tools, the data collected, and the Big Data/machine-learning/AI tools used to optimize profits extracted from selling the data. These integrated platforms have become some of the most profitable and powerful assets in the global economy.

Meanwhile, autocratic regimes are busy acquiring surveillance platforms that add data streams from facial-recognition cameras to databases on citizens, enhancing their profiling and targeting of dissidents.

While the corporate owners of AI tools never miss an opportunity to promote the happy story that AI will improve everyone's lives, in reality is AI is a highly profitable asset they are optimizing to maximize profits. The only way to extract maximum profits from AI is to maintain ownership or control of AI, which means limiting the public's access to AI-based tools. Since AI is a key source of value, then restricting ownership and control to a few corporations means income and wealth inequality will only widen - the profits from owning proprietary AI tools will flow to a handful of platforms while the bottom 95% slide further into poverty.

Thus this slide into poverty by the masses has three sources: first, their access to AI-powered capital is limited by platform dominance of this form of capital, and secondly, automation devalues their labor, and third, AI commoditizes labor that was previously immune to automation.

Increasing Wealth Inequality

Societies fragmented by rising income-wealth inequality eventually fracture, destroying the foundations of wealth. Just as cancer cells that are too successful end up killing the host and themselves, corporations that are too successful at hoarding control of the most profitable forms of capital will kill the "host" social order that they need to exist—killing the goose that laid the golden eggs.

These platforms hire commoditized labor at low wages for assembly of goods, delivery of services and distribution (fulfillment warehouses, drivers, etc.), and automate whatever tasks can be profitably automated (warehouse robots, AI agents, etc.). This is the logic of maximizing profit: eliminate one of the primary costs—labor—to increase profits even as sales stagnate. Like a cancer cell that reproduces without any awareness of the self-destructive logic of runaway reproduction, the question of how a consumer economy can function as employment declines and wages stagnate is beyond the corporate focus on short-term profits.

This is yet another *ontological contradiction*: the way to maximize profits is to ruthlessly eliminate labor costs, and leave it to some other institution to create the high-wage secure jobs needed to buy all the goods and services being sold by platforms.

In reality there are no institutions or sectors capable of generating tens of millions of high-wage secure jobs. Low-profit legacy enterprises (small business, manufacturing, retail, etc.) are struggling to invest in commodity-automation tools to slash human labor costs just to keep afloat, and governments globally are facing stagnating revenue as demographics turn negative (the workforce is shrinking as the cohort of retirees explodes). The destabilizing forces of financialization are finally reversing the 40-year dynamic of virtuous expansion of debt and consumption into a self-reinforcing dynamic of speculative excess, debt renunciation and insolvency.

The most profitable solution for the corporate owners of AI is Universal Basic Income (UBI), a mass distribution of enough monthly cash to every household so outstanding loans can be paid and corporate goods and services can be purchased.

If consumers have no money beyond the basics of survival, then the value of data collected by platforms drops precipitously: it makes no financial sense to pay a premium for data to influence consumers who have little disposable income. (Recall that the top 10% of households account for roughly half of all income and consumption.)

There is another *ontological contradiction* that impacts the class of technocrats who seek elite employment in the corporate platforms or their ancillary sectors (regulatory agencies, legal services, software programming, global marketing, etc.): the class seeking elite employment is expanding far faster than the employment opportunities and the economy as a whole. This dynamic guarantees system-wide disappointment and frustration within the highly educated class that was raised to consider elite employment as either a birthright (i.e. the children of elites) or the just desserts of winning the meritocracy battle (gaining entry to elites universities, earning advanced degrees, etc.).

This dashing of the high expectations of this class has political consequences: these are not people who will accept impoverishment as their lot in life, nor blame themselves for their failures. They did everything that was expected of them and their disappointment reflects a systemic failure that can't be attributed to personal inadequacies. This awareness of the structural flaws in a system rigged to protect elites is political dynamite.

Systems and Commoditization

We are now in a position to understand the destructive forces unleashed by commoditization and systems that are rigged to maintain elite dominance. Both are riddled with *ontological contradictions*: the only way the system can reliably output elite dominance is to limit real-world feedback loops, a limitation that fatally destabilizes the system by stripping it of the feedback needed to maintain stability.

Commoditization drives profit margins to zero, forcing enterprises to automate tasks to eliminate labor costs. The labor that cannot be profitably automated is either commoditized (i.e. broken down into tasks that can be performed by workforces around the world), or specialized to the point that it can be automated. Meanwhile, the highly educated workforce expecting elite positions expands, generating frustrations that eventually manifest as political unrest.

This system is intrinsically unstable, socially and politically.

The distribution/data collection corporations profiting from ownership of capital-intensive AI tools have a strong self-interest in maintaining ownership/control of these tools, preventing their distribution to enterprises lower down the wealth-power pyramid. As ordinary capital and labor have been commoditized, they've lost value, leaving quasi-monopolistic data collection and AI tools as the most profitable forms of capital. Everyone with only ordinary capital and labor is losing ground as costs rise; only the few who own proprietary AI tools are gaining ground. This widening of wealth and income inequality is also intrinsically unstable.

The quasi-monopolistic platforms have tremendous incentives to secure their ownership and control of these scarce forms of capital. To do so, they must keep these tools from being commoditized, and they must erect regulatory and network-effect 'moats' around these core profit sources. To accomplish this, they must rig the system to output their dominance, and this requires eliminating or marginalizing feedback loops of information that are outside of their control.

The net result is a nexus of power over all feedback loops: corporate, state and mass media information flows are all controlled to limit undesirable feedback. The faces of power change, but the structure and output (elite dominance) remain static. As noted earlier, if the inputs and processes of the current system remain unchanged, the only possible output is elite dominance.

In effect, the corporate platforms must hoard the most profitable capital and talent, depriving the rest of the economy of the capital and talent needed to expand productivity. This dynamic accelerates income-wealth inequality, which in turn accelerates social and economic fragmentation, which fuels social discord that leads to breakdown and collapse.

Like cancer cells, the corporate platforms are winning the competition for resources but are unaware that their victory over the healthy cells will soon kill their host, destroying the wealth and power they sought to perpetuate at the expense of everyone else.

The Unique Power to Create Money Out of Thin Air

Our monetary system creates new money in two ways: first of all, the central bank (the Federal Reserve in the U.S.) creates currency with a few keystrokes and buys Treasury bonds, mortgage-backed securities or other financial assets with the new money. They now own an asset of equal value to the money they created out of thin air.

The second way is for commercial banks to issue loans such as mortgages to borrowers. In our *fractional reserve system*, only $5 of each $100 loan is cash; the other $95 is new money created out of thin air, backed by the market value of the home that serves as collateral for the mortgage.

The key features of this system are that *money is borrowed into existence*, and interest is due on the money that has been borrowed into existence. The borrower must pay the mortgage lender some percentage of the principal and interest on the balance of the loan. Should the borrower not pay the principal and interest, the loan is in default.

Should the mortgage lender foreclose on the defaulted mortgage, the house will be sold to retire the mortgage balance. If the mortgage is $250,000 and the house only fetches $200,000, the lender suffers a $50,000 loss, and the money supply decreases by $50,000: $50,000 of the money that was created by the mortgage being originated vanishes back into thin air.

Notice that in these two examples, the new money is backed by collateral—a Treasury bond or a house. But this is not a requirement; money that is completely disconnected from any real-world asset can be loaned into existence. When someone charges a luxury vacation on a credit card, the money created by this loan isn't backed by any physical collateral, because the money was spent on experiences, not assets.

Increasing the supply of money doesn't increase the real-world resources available for purchase. If the money supply is increased ten-fold overnight, $10 of gasoline will then cost $100. Our $100 won't buy ten times more gasoline as $10 bought a month ago; it buys the same amount of gasoline.

Creating more money out of thin air doesn't make us collectively wealthier, it only makes those who get the money wealthier. Compare two systems: in the first, everyone can create new money on their home printer. In the second, only a select handful of private banks can create money out of thin air. In the first system, the purchasing power of this everyone-can-create-it money soon drops to zero. In the second system, insiders can create new money for themselves and a few cronies, and use this money to buy up income-producing assets. These few will become richer while the entire system becomes poorer, as any expansion of the money supply reduces the purchasing power of all existing money.

Let's say a financier borrows $1 billion from a private bank at 2% annual interest, and uses this new money to buy a corporate bond paying 4% interest annually. After paying the interest on the loan, the financier nets $20,000,000 annually. The bank earns 2% and the financier earns 2% on money of which only 5% existed prior to the loan.

The financier produced no new goods or services or innovations, but does get to enjoy the $20,000,000 in unearned income (minus taxes of course, which will be minimal if the financier originated the loan in an offshore tax-haven.)

In the happy fiction promoted by the elites benefiting from this scheme, money is only borrowed into existence to bring brilliant innovations to life and enable hard-working households to buy a family home. In the real world, money is created to benefit the banks and the few financiers and corporations with access to the money being created and distributed. These entities use the newly created money to buy up income-producing assets with the added potential of capital gains such as home mortgages, profitable enterprises, stocks and bonds. This income enriches them in two ways: it provides income which can be used to buy more assets, and it generates more capital, since owning an income stream increases net worth.

The newly created money flows to the few at the expense of the many; a select few get the income generated by the assets being purchased, while the many suffer a subtle loss in the purchasing power of their money, since any increase in the money supply that isn't matched by a corresponding increase in the supply of goods, services and resources devalues existing money.

This system is intrinsically unstable for several reasons. Since money is borrowed into existence, interest is due. As the money supply expands, so does the interest due. If income (wages) stagnate, then an increasing percentage of household income goes to paying interest on household debt, leaving less disposable income to save/invest or spend on consumables.

To compensate for this reduction in disposable income, households borrow more, creating a feedback of rising debt and interest payments. Once interest and essentials take all the household income and the household can no longer afford to borrow more money, household consumption drops and the consumer economy collapses.

To stave off this collapse, central banks drop interest rates to near zero and increase credit limits, so consumers and businesses can continue to borrow more money. But this reduction in interest rates to near zero effectively destroys the core function of capital, which is to earn a return that is correlated to risk: the higher the risk, the greater the return. At near-zero rates of interest, lenders are losing money once inflation is factored in, and they receive nothing for the higher risks that go hand in hand with explosive increases of debt.

As households and businesses become over-indebted, the risk of default increases. In an economy undistorted by central bank manipulation, lenders would charge higher interest rates as the risks of default rose. But trapped in a low interest rate world by central banks, to earn a positive return on capital banks lend to speculative ventures, greatly increasing the risk that capital will suffer losses.

In effect, to keep the debt-dependent economy afloat, central banks have eradicated low-risk returns on capital, forcing capital into high-risk investments as the only way to earn a positive yield.

However, the strategy of lowering interest rates to near zero so consumers and businesses can stay afloat by borrowing more money has an expiration date. Stagnant incomes can only support so much debt before default becomes inevitable.

The last gasp of this intrinsically unstable system is for the central state to become the borrower of last resort, borrowing trillions of dollars annually to distribute UBI so households can continue to service their debts and spend enough to keep the consumer economy from imploding. But all this will do is push the day of reckoning forward a bit, since this vast expansion of government debt will devalue the money and the rising interest payments will crowd out other state spending. Eventually, the state will be borrowing not just trillions to fund UBI but trillions in interest due on the ballooning public debt.

Meanwhile, since capital has no way to earn any kind of return on low-risk investments, it flows into speculative asset bubbles which eventually and inevitably pop, destroying all the phantom wealth borrowed into existence by central and private banks.

Given the inputs and processes—the way money is created and distributed—the only possible outputs of this system are rising wealth inequality, increasing dependence on debt to keep the system afloat, and perverse incentives to speculate as the only way to earn a positive return on capital.

Such a perverse system will impoverish everyone when it finally collapses under its own weight.

This is why I say: *if we don't change the way we create and distribute money, we've changed nothing.*

Multiple Points of Failure in the Power Structure

The output of our current socio-political-economic system is the self-perpetuating structure of elite power over the masses. Every one of its many ontological contradictions and intrinsic sources of instability are potential points of failure. We can play a parlor game of guessing which one fails first, but the point here is the system is inherently unstable and cannot be rendered stable by the usual cosmetic reforms. The only way to make the system stable is to change the inputs and processes, thereby changing the outputs.

Our existing system is impoverished and impoverishing. Like cancer, its narrowly defined success dooms the host and itself to destruction.

To preserve what's left of natural capital and restore some stability to society and the economy, we need to institutionalize new relationships between capital, labor and the natural world that recognize that all that we've ignored as if it doesn't exist *does in fact exist* and is vitally important to the well-being and survival of all of us – elites included.

Section Six: New Relationships between Capital, Labor and the Natural World

We began by exploring what we're measuring in misleading ways, what we're not measuring, and what's being ignored as if it doesn't exist. It turns out a great many things which we don't account for—i.e. accept as inputs—do exist after all, and are of critical importance.

Next we explored the appealing fantasy that robots and AI will effortlessly enrich us all by performing most or all human labor and generating limitless profits as far as the eye can see. We discovered that robots will only do what maximizes profits for the elites who control capital and power, so robots and AI will be busy burning down rainforests, draining aquifers, overusing pesticides, micro-targeting consumers and speculating in debt-fueled asset bubbles, maximizing profits for elites and maintaining the elite's dominance as the desired output of the entire socio-political-economic system.

We also examined the fantasy, in terms of costs and real-world reliability, of commoditized devices—and discovered that robots and the physical machinery of AI will end up as just more waste in the Landfill Economy, alongside all the other defective, poorly made and engineered consumer products. We found that *Smart Houses* and the entire Internet of Things is horrendously costly to create yet produces little positive output, the very definition of a waste of capital.

As for generating limitless profits, we discovered that commoditization reduces profits to near-zero, and all the components of robotics and AI are rapidly being commoditized, meaning profits will soon fall to near-zero, just like all other commoditized components.

Next, we surveyed costs and types of capital that aren't being measured, and found that if we accepted all these costs and losses of capital as inputs, we are getting poorer, not richer: the expansion of financial wealth is just an illusion that serves the self-perpetuating power of elites.

We concluded that technology and markets are like Natural Selection; they have no internal *teleology*, i.e. no preset purpose or goals. Technology and markets won't automatically conserve the planet's resources or distribute them fairly or create livelihoods for hundreds of millions of people. In our current system, the inputs and processes, including technology and markets, are controlled to output the self-perpetuating dominance of elites and maximize their financial profits. These are the only possible outputs of the system given its current limited inputs and processes. If we want different goals and outputs, we must change the inputs and processes.

We then considered the intrinsic instability of our socio-political-economic system and its many ontological contradictions, each of which is a point of failure that will eventually collapse the system. We found that our system is analogous to highly successful cancer cells which outcompete healthy cells in the battle for resources. The cancer cells have one measure of success, their reproduction. As a result, the cancer cells are blind to the consequence of their success: the demise of their host and thus their own demise. In our system, the output goal is financial profits. Our system is equally blind to the consequences of its narrowly defined success: the depletion of natural capital and the ultimate demise of the entire system.

Clearly, we need a new system, one that institutionalizes new relationships among the natural world (natural capital), human labor, and all other forms of capital—financial, social, cultural, intellectual and all other forms of intangible capital.

The output of a system is established by the inputs the system accepts and the processes it performs. As explained earlier, our system restricts the inputs and processes to generate the elites' desired output—their continued dominance and the maximization of only their financial profits. But limiting feedback loops to get the desired output fatally destabilizes the system, because feedback from the real world is the essential dynamic in stable systems.

So our first step is to remove the lock on outputs—that the system must be rigged to sustain elite dominance, regardless of any costs or consequences—and focus on accepting a new, expansive and flexible range of feedback loops. This same flexibility must be given to processes.

If we want a system that recognizes natural capital, biodiversity, democracy, truth, security, fairness and human livelihoods as valuable, then we'll have to define and accept inputs that reflect these values.

If we want a realistic accounting of costs, we'll have to accept inputs that measure all the external costs currently ignored as if they don't exist. We'll have to accept new inputs that reflect all the forms of capital that are now suffering catastrophic losses as an (unrecognized) output of the current system.

If we don't want to follow the successful cancer cells to self-destruction, we need to broaden the definition of profit from narrowly defined financial profit that ignores all external costs to a much more accurate accounting of profit that includes utility to communities, conservation of resources and biodiversity, efficiency, and the accumulation of social and other forms of intangible capital.

We also need a new way to create and distribute money that doesn't simply serve self-perpetuating elites.

Incentives to Designing a Better System

To design a new system, we must start with the assumptions and incentives that are built into the inputs, processes and feedback loops. Most idealistic systems focus on defining the output (for example, justice, economic security, happiness, etc.) but neglect to examine what the system rewards / punishes and the resulting consequences of participants acting on those incentives.

The desired incentives may be undermined by implicit, unstated incentives. Thus communism defined the goal output as everyone working to the best of their ability and sharing in the proceeds. However, this contrasts with basic human nature with its implicit incentives to favor oneself and one's family and friends, and to reap windfalls when possible. If power is centralized, i.e. owned by elites, human nature has implicit incentives to use this power over others to benefit one's inner circle at the expense of everyone else.

With this is mind, it's clear that defining idealistic outputs is the path to exploitation and failure. Instead, we need to institutionalize incentives that self-perpetuate the health and stability of the system by eliminating centralization and participants' ability to rig inputs in favor themselves at the expense of everyone else.

In other words, the system must be designed so that centralizing power and securing unearned privileges are impossible.

Since money is a claim on inherently limited natural resources, let's start by designing a new system of creating and distributing money. Rather than grant a monopoly on money creation to the elite (central and private banks), let's grant a monopoly on money creation to *human labor that's organized to serve the needs and scarcities of local communities*. This is a *labor-backed currency*, and since it is issued as payment for human labor that serves communities, it isn't borrowed into existence. Rather, it expands the money supply in direct correlation to the expansion of goods and services within the community economy.

To secure this currency from tampering or centralization, let's automate its issuance according to strict guidelines and make it a cryptocurrency, i.e. a currency that is generated and distributed by a network of servers rather than a central bank or government. This currency is intrinsically decentralized and intrinsically resistant to centralization. Since the issuance is controlled by the fundamental design of the currency, there are no human agents that can be influenced, bribed, threatened or bought.

Let's further stipulate that this labor-backed cryptocurrency is open source, so any meddling to serve an elite cannot be hidden from view.

Since this currency is paid only to labor serving local communities, who decides what projects qualify as serving the community? To make centralization and coercion impossible, the decision-making process is embedded in self-organizing community groups that must follow democratic processes and project guidelines to qualify for payments of the new currency. Any groups that don't meet the standards receive no payments. By instantiating the guidelines in smart software (i.e. AI), the guidelines will be applied equally to all groups.

In effect, these groups are *self-organizing democratically managed enterprises* whose dual mandate is filling local scarcities and managing local resources in a sustainable manner. Profit includes not just financial profits, but also more flexible, expansive inputs of utility, frugality, efficiency and conservation,

To ensure a multitude of transparent feedback loops in the system, any participant can start their own community enterprise, provided they follow the guidelines. Thus no group has a hold over participants or the community. Groups which fail for any reason dissolve and are replaced by new groups. This churn of low-level experimentation, failure and success provides the necessary real-world feedback required for systemic stability. This is the systemic strength of free enterprise: new enterprises arise as experiments that either outcompete existing businesses or fail.

The importance of this structure cannot be overstated: the goal of the system is to ensure the accuracy, authenticity and legitimacy of inputs and processes that serve the goals of the entire system, leaving the outputs to express the variability required for system stability. Some groups will succeed, some will fail, some projects will attract multiple groups that coordinate their efforts, some groups will remain small and marginal, and others will expand rapidly. All of this variability is characteristic of healthy ecosystems.

What projects qualify as serving the community? We can rephrase this question as: how do we define profit? The basic dynamic of economics is supply and demand, and so filling local scarcities is a core community project. Filling local scarcities is thus inherently profitable. In this larger sense, utility and frugal management of labor and capital are profitable in this new system.

If there is a local shortage of food, the groups should focus on filling that scarcity, or, if that isn't possible, they should focus on creating goods and services that can be traded for food that other groups have in surplus. If housing is scarce, then groups should concentrate capital and labor on constructing or rehabilitating housing, and so on. Since there will likely be a variety of local scarcities, various groups will likely decide to focus (i.e. specialize) on filling a specific scarcity. Some will be more successful than others, and as existing scarcities are addressed, groups can turn their resources on less pressing scarcities.

The second basic dynamic of economics is that natural capital is not inexhaustible; therefore sustainable management of local natural capital is the primary form of profit. Once maintaining biodiversity becomes a measurable input, then sustainable management of fisheries, forests, etc. becomes more profitable than clearcutting and overfishing, which only maximize profits in the current system.

This new system establishes new relationships between the natural world, labor and capital. Since money isn't borrowed into existence, interest doesn't accrue except when groups save their earnings and lend it to other groups to aid the completion of their community projects. Since the money supply only expands as the supply of goods and services expand, the monetary claims on resources cannot be arbitrarily increased.

Once all forms of capital are measured and accepted as inputs, all the forms of capital that are (thoughtlessly destroyed in our current system) will finally have value.

Rather than drive a race to the bottom, the commoditization of technologies will become a form of low-cost capital that can be distributed to community enterprises to help fill local scarcities. Instead of becoming the latest form of planned-obsolescence waste dumped in landfills, commoditized tools can be used to design repairable and sustainable machinery that simply isn't profitable in strictly financial terms. The most efficient uses of these technologies can be shared, rather than hoarded by quasi-monopolistic corporations.

Will the self-perpetuating elites hoarding capital and power gladly relinquish their control? Of course not. Like successful cancer cells, they will cling on to their control until they collapse the entire system and destroy themselves.

As F. Buckminster Fuller famously observed, *"To change something, build a new model that makes the existing model obsolete."*

Former CEO of Intel Andy Grove addressed technology's role in this obsoleting of the current system: *"Not all problems have a technological answer, but when they do, that is the more lasting solution."*

Many of humanity's problems do not have a technological solution, or at least the low-cost, painless variety that populate techno-fantasies. Energy costs are unlikely to fall to near-zero, for all the reasons described earlier, and the current economic system is incapable of providing higher wage jobs for the millions of people being displaced by automation. Since profits will decline as profitable sectors are commoditized, paying people high enough levels of UBI to support current consumption out of tax revenues is also not possible. Borrowing the trillions of dollars needed to fund UBI will collapse the monetary system since this vast expansion of the money supply won't be matched by a corresponding expansion in goods and services.

The massive losses of natural and intangible capital described in previous chapters will not be reversed for the simple reason that these forms of capital aren't recognized and thus do not exist in the current system.

For all these reasons, technology can't save the current system from itself. Preserving our current elite-dominated, debt-dependent Landfill Economy is not an option.

One option (the one currently in place) is to follow the lead of successful cancer cells and keep doing what we're doing—maximizing profits for elites while depleting all the forms of capital that the current system doesn't even acknowledge, much less accept as inputs—and kill the host, i.e. the current socio-political-economic system.

The other (better) option is to obsolete this system by establishing a new decentralized power structure which distributes its own money to those who perform labor helping to fill scarcities and needs in their community. This new power structure does not need to replace the existing power structure; it need only co-exist while the current power structure self-destructs.

The technology needed to operate such a decentralized, self-funding economy on a global scale already exists. The technology of cryptocurrencies is well-established, and the additional layer of software required by the labor-backed cryptocurrency proposed here is well within reach of commoditized software tools.

The software required to institutionalize the democratically governed community enterprises and marketplaces for the goods and services produced by the enterprises is no different than existing private-sector platforms.

As for starting to measure what has not been getting measured, and adding these new feedback loops as inputs, the process of trial and error and experimentation is also well-established.

I've outlined such an alternative system-- The Community Labor Integrated Money Economy (CLIME) --in a previous book, *A Radically Beneficial World: Automation, Technology and Creating Jobs for All.* I invite you to explore the entire system in greater detail, with the understanding that my proposal is a starting point in a long process of experimentation, feedback and improvement.

Humans are very resistant to change. We like a bit of novelty, but only within the safe boundaries of entertainment. It's understandable that we want the positive outputs of the current system to remain unchanged, and we want assurances that all the outputs we currently enjoy will remain unchanged.

But here's the thing about systems: if we lock the output and restrict the inputs and processes to give us the desired output, we fatally destabilize the system because we're depriving it of the feedback and variability it needs to remain stable.

This is just like the cancer cells locking in their desired output—continuing to outcompete healthy cells to maximize reproduction. The cancer cells are so successful at locking in their output that they kill the host and themselves.

If we enable the expansion of inputs and feedback, and enable flexibility, adaptability and variability in processes, we assure the stability of the system, not the stability of the outputs. We can't predict what the outputs will be of a system that accounts for all the external costs the current system ignores, or that measures, however imperfectly, the loss of biodiversity and intangible capital.

We can't predict how much energy we'll each have access to, or how many resources we'll each have to consume. But we can predict that the system won't ignore traumatizing losses of irreplaceable capital, and that it won't be rigged to output the dominance of self-perpetuating, self-serving elites.

We can also predict that money will no longer be created to benefit elites, and that it won't be borrowed into existence to benefit banks. We can predict that the labor-backed cryptocurrency will be connected with the real world of people producing goods and services that fill scarcities and meet needs.

We can't predict what tasks may be done by robots and AI, but we can predict that human labor will still be valued and compensated, that this labor will be purposeful and meaningful, and that the labor and the compensation will enable individuals, households and communities to accumulate capital. We can also predict that the capital of commoditized robotics and AI will be available to every community enterprise in the network, so whatever benefits do flow from commoditized automation and AI will flow not to a handful of global corporations but to everyone participating in this new system.

Systems aren't impacted by our emotional response to their collapse. Systems stripped of real-world feedback, variability, flexibility and adaptability are intrinsically unstable and will collapse regardless of our feelings, hopes, beliefs and fantasies. Our disbelief in the inevitability of the collapse of unstable systems won't magically save the system, nor will our furious arguments that 'the system is stable' change the fact the system is fatally destabilized by its structure and what it doesn't accept as inputs.

The technologies of robotics, automation and AI won't change the power structure via some sort of teleological magic, or magically stabilize a rigged, blindly self-destructive system. That's up to us. Only we can choose the values and goals that our systems manifest. Only we can realize we need a new system and set ourselves the task of creating it.

Section Seven: Where Will Your Capital Flourish?

Now that we've surveyed the costs and forms of capital the status quo doesn't measure (much less recognize) and sketched out a less distorted and more sustainable alternative system, we've come to the big question: *what does all this mean for me and my life*? What does it mean to an individual who has to work in our current system with all its perverse incentives and dysfunctional blindness?

Assessing Our Current Wealth: Richer or Poorer?

Our broader understanding of capital, costs and systems enables us to conduct a comprehensive personal reckoning: where are we putting our time, energy, and capital, and what's our return for this all-in investment of our life? We are now equipped to assess all the forms of capital we own or have access to, and what types of capital we don't have but want to have. We're also able to account for all the real costs we're incurring, including declines of intangible capital.

Once we assess our personal capital and costs, we may find we're actually richer than we thought: we might not be financially well-off, but we may be rich in skills and experience (human capital), in friendships, personal connections and trustworthy networks (social capital), in cultural traditions and values, in access to green spaces and natural beauty, in proximity to markets and transport, in access to functional, flexible local economies and systems of governance, in authenticity and integrity, in a healthy mix of work, play, socializing and learning, and in *agency*, i.e. control of our life and capital.

Or we may find that despite an outsized financial net worth, we're deeply impoverished: lonely, without any intimate, trustworthy friends; alienated from our family; addicted to our phone, social media and self-medication; mired in a deranging lifestyle focused on money, status and accumulating "likes;" stuck in a corrupt, dysfunctional economy; exposed to toxic air and water; surrounded by consumer luxury but far from any natural beauty; living a life devoid of authenticity and integrity, a life of distrust, angst and poor mental and physical health, and lacking any meaningful control of our life.

Or we may find a complex mix of positives and negatives.

Once we have a new broader understanding of our own personal capital, costs and systems, we can make more informed decisions about where best to invest our time, energy and capital to accumulate what we might call *full-spectrum wealth*, i.e. all forms of capital, rather than just financial capital. We are now also better prepared to assess our own self-interests in an economy designed to enrich the few at the expense of the many, an economy distorted by what isn't measured or incentivized.

Measuring Our Full Spectrum Wealth

Since we don't currently measure all forms of capital, the non-financial costs of these decisions are hidden from our accounting, but not from our lived experience. We feel the burdens of debt as chronic stress and we sense we're not getting ahead despite doing everything that we were told would make us financially successful and thus happy, as financial security is presumed to the core ingredient of happiness. (This is the primary assumption of our entire system.) This system we take for granted—of working fulltime for an employer and borrowing enormous sums of money for college, housing, transport and leisure—is impoverishing if we add up the costs that aren't measured and the non-financial capital that's being squandered to service the debt.

Our economy incentivizes developing a specialized skill and selling one's skill and time to the highest bidder, an employer who seeks to maximize profit by extracting as much value as possible from us. This requires the employee to work fulltime and often make extra effort, such as answering emails on the weekend, agreeing to work overtime as needed, and so on, all without additional pay.

We're presented with what amounts to an all-or-nothing proposal: the only way we can maximize the value of our labor is to take on a heavy burden of student loans for a college credential in order to get a better paying job, and then use our future earnings as collateral for loans to buy a car, a house and all the trappings of a middle class lifestyle: vacations, lessons for the children and so on.

The conventional context of this appraisal is psychological, because the sources of our anxiety, stress and disillusionment are internal. We assume our unhappiness or lack of financial success stems from our lack of spiritual awareness (mindfulness); our imperfect career choices; our personality flaws; our inability to master the winner-take-most competitions of investing and work, and so on. If we're unhappy and falling behind, the fault lies not with the system, but with our inadequacies.

This focus is understandable, given that individual decisions, efforts and values largely dictate the financial outcomes in our system (stipulating, of course, that sheer luck can trump everything else). An individual who acquires scarce skills and markets them effectively, who lives by positive values (frugality, integrity, trustworthiness, flexibility, compassion, ability to defer gratification, etc.), who marries well (i.e. partners with a spouse with similar values, work ethic and income) and stays married, minimizes debt and accepts prudent risks to reap outsized gains (which our system incentivizes) will generate much higher financial returns than an individual who doesn't acquire desirable skills, has slipshod values, makes poor decisions, indulges in instant gratification, runs up large debts and doesn't marry well.

But individual decisions and values don't change the system. Once we account for the full spectrum of capital and costs, we realize the system itself is dysfunctional, and to expect those trapped in this blindly destructive system to maintain a healthy life is tragically absurd.

Yes, we can change our outcomes by changing our lives, values, skills, locale, etc. But self-help won't change the system's innate destructiveness. All we can do is limit the system's negative impact on ourselves and our households.

Once we step out of the self-help frame of reference and start measuring capital, we have a new and more objective context for assessing what we're sacrificing (i.e. the opportunity costs of what else we could be doing with our capital and time), what we're risking and what our investment is yielding—not just in financial terms but in the full spectrum of costs and capital.

A simple thought experiment reveals the limits of financial capital. Let's imagine an individual is given a wallet stuffed with cash, a pocketful of gold and a digital wallet with bitcoin, and dropped into a desert devoid of human settlement. There's nobody to trade with, and nothing to buy; this unfortunate individual will die wealthy in financial terms but unable to buy the water and food needed to survive.

In other words, money only has value in a market economy with people with real-world goods and services they're willing to trade for money.

Viewed from the perspective of intangible capital, in many ways our economy is a desert in which the highest value forms of capital cannot be bought. We've been trained to believe that money can buy anything and everything, but it can't buy fulfillment, trust, clean air in a toxic environment (cans of "fresh air" are a risible "market solution"), or food and water in an uninhabited desert. Money only has value if it can secure ownership or access to the highest value forms of capital.

The Highest Forms of Capital

What are these highest value forms of capital? We can break tangible and intangible capital into four broad categories:

1. Our **intangible internal capital**: our values (frugality, integrity, trustworthiness, flexibility, compassion, ability to defer gratification, etc.), communication skills, emotional intelligence, ability to learn quickly, situational awareness, intuition, decision-making skills, generosity, and so on. These are what we would want in a spouse, business partner, or friend, and we certainly want them if we're a friend to ourselves. (As Abraham Lincoln observed: "If I have lost every other friend on earth, I shall at least have one friend left, and that friend shall be down inside of me."). Even if we lose all our financial capital, we still possess our internal capital.

2. The **tangible and intangible *societal capital*** available to us: the infrastructure of roadways, trains, subways and utilities; the cultural capital of transparent, effective governance, the security of our property rights and civil liberties; the freedom to dissent and move freely; the financial capital of credit, clear pathways to self-employment and entrepreneurship with open markets for our labor and what we produce; access to public libraries and

learning resources; access to healthcare; the environmental capital of clean air and water and public parks and open spaces for recreation, and so on.

3. Equally important is the **system's integrity and *resilience***, i.e. the ability to maintain these forms of societal capital in what is termed *de-growth* (usually written as *DeGrowth)*, extended or even permanent declines in the resources and income available to sustain society's infrastructure. Resilience is an especially difficult type of capital to measure, as it manifests when resources and income trend downward and do not quickly recover previous levels. Resilience requires flexibility, adaptability, innovation and a high tolerance for the failures that result from experimentation and *creative destruction*, the collapse of institutions triggered by costs exceeding available income, or by innovations that obsolete existing structures.

Few civilizations survive DeGrowth because elites and vested interests (insiders) cling to ossified, unsustainable institutional sources of their privilege and power. I address these dynamics in my book *Pathfinding our Destiny: Preventing the Final Fall of our Democratic Republic.*

Put another way: how vulnerable to disruption are these forms of societal capital?

4. Your **own income and *economic capital***, which includes marketable skills, tools, social capital (such as a network of trusted work collaborators), entrepreneurial experience, currency and other forms of money (precious metals, cryptocurrencies, etc.), land, buildings, vehicles, and perhaps most importantly, our mental and physical health and well-being, as well as *control of our lives, capital and decisions*. If we are trapped in an unfavorable situation and unable to progress and unable to leave it, we are impoverished in a most profound way.

A full accounting of our capital would include all the forms of societal capital we can access; an assessment of the integrity and resilience of this societal capital, i.e. the risks that access might become limited or restricted due to social decay or disorder, or costs that become unaffordable to most residents; our intangible internal capital, our economic capital and our agency and freedom of movement, i.e. *control of our lives, capital and decisions*.

Viewing all this from the perspective of capital rather than from the viewpoint of psychology and self-help ("the problem is this long list of your weaknesses and flaws; if only you were better at XYZ you'd be happier and more successful"), the next step is to ask if your capital is earning the highest possible return in security, full-spectrum wealth and well-being. If it isn't, then what other opportunities are available where your capital will be treated more favorably?

Banker Walter Wriston famously observed that "Capital will always go where it's welcome and stay where it's well treated. Capital is not just money. It's also talent and ideas. They, too, will go where they're welcome and stay where they are well treated." This idea has been summarized as *Capital goes where it is treated best.*

Capital goes not just where it is welcome, but where it is secure, and where it has the widest access to other forms of capital and the widest range of opportunities. Since our capital includes our health and control of our lives, we might summarize the goal as: we want to invest our capital to progress by accumulating all forms of capital, but most importantly the highest value forms of capital.

Where Will My Capital Flourish?

In broad brush, economies need the following: energy sources, the production of goods and services, circulation (transport and currency), trade, markets, institutionalized protections of property and intellectual rights, and fairly administered tax collection to spread the costs of shared infrastructure and legal protections among all participants. The greater the freedom of movement of currency, capital, energy, goods, information, knowledge and people, the greater the variety and velocity of economic activity.

As a general rule, the more decentralized the economy, the greater the diversity and velocity of its economic activity. The more centralized the economy, the greater its concentration of wealth and power, the more corrupt its governance, and the lower its diversity, activity and opportunity. The greater the control by centralized elites and vested interests, the less control by everyone else.

Financial capital can flow around the world with just a few keystrokes on a keyboard. Humans tends to be embedded in locales with ties to family, friends, colleagues, homes, neighborhoods, and so on. It's not easy to move our lives from one place to another, and any move is fraught with risk: we might not like the new locale, and our capital might not go as far or buy as we'd anticipated.

We naturally resist moving, but here is the question we must answer: how much of our capital is *stranded* in unproductive uses or *dormant*, sitting in a low-yield account? This includes not just financial capital but our talents, skills, etc. that are dormant or stranded. We might phrase this more provocatively: where will I be free to make the kind of progress I want to make? Or, put another way, where will my capital be welcomed and valued?

A major focus of this book is on costs, both the financial kind we measure and those we don't measure. As someone who has burned out twice due to overwork and the stresses of juggling business and personal challenges, the internal costs of navigating a deranging, dysfunctional system are very real to me. If integrity, well-being and natural beauty are scarce in our lives, we are paying a very high cost whether we measure it or not. Our minds and bodies foot the bill, so to speak, as our health and well-being degrade and collapse.

Regardless of how much money we have, if the costs of living maintaining a specific lifestyle in a specific place are crushing us, whatever yield we're receiving on our capital won't stave off an eventual reckoning in which our health and well-being are bankrupted. As noted earlier, the most valuable forms of capital cannot be commoditized or marketed, and so they can't be bought.

Locales with sclerotic, high-cost institutions that serve vested interests controlling highly centralized nodes of power and wealth are most vulnerable to DeGrowth. Locales with flexible, responsive, low-cost decentralized institutions that serve the public interest are much more likely to find ways to maintain critical infrastructure when revenues and resources trend lower.

Tradeoffs, Risk and Return

Just as there is no easy, foolproof way to account for all the complexities of capital in all its forms, there is no perfectly risk-free investment of capital that doesn't require the sacrifice of other opportunities. Risk and return are connected. Low risk yields low returns. High risk yields a greater potential for failure but also the potential for outsized returns.

The past twenty years of central bank intervention in financial markets has created the illusion that financial risks have been vanquished because the Federal Reserve and other central banks will always step in and "save the day" if markets start falling. But central banks are not all-powerful; they can no more rescind risk than can rescind gravity. With interest rates falling into negative territory around the world, central bank policies are hitting the wall of diminishing returns: rather than generate a positive economic response, lowering interest rates is worsening the malaise.

Rather than stabilizing the global financial system, decades of increasing intervention have increased systemic risk by making markets overly-dependent on central banks. This dependency on distortions has made the system fragile and prone to system-wide disruptions that more intervention can't fix.

Every investment of capital requires tradeoffs. If we commit ourselves to maximizing financial earnings, we're trading other forms of capital for this increase in financial capital: we're trading our time, agency, focus and energy, and racking up opportunity costs as all the other options we could have invested in go by the wayside.

What forms of capital are worth more to us than other forms? This is a highly individual assessment. While we all need enough money to buy the essentials of life and some measure of agency, some people are willing to strip their financial expenses to the bone to enable them to invest their time and energy in other forms of capital.

This greatly complicates our assessment and our reckoning: not only is it difficult to identify all the forms of capital in our lives, and then assign some sort of value to each one, it's difficult to prioritize them in our own lives. We naturally want to be rich in everything: money, security, social status, time, beauty, health and so on. But in the real world, everything requires investments, tradeoffs, and a calculation of risk and return.

That said, we have to start somewhere, and listing all our capital is a good start. Putting the list in order of priority is an exercise which forces us to question how much of what we value comes from society (whatever increases our status in our social circle, for example) and what is core to us as individuals.

We all know everyone makes tradeoffs to earn money, but how much are we trading away? Approaching the question systemically by listing all the tradeoffs we're making and prioritizing the list is one way of establishing what we value most and what we're willing to let go of.

Next, we can constructively look at our lives as a system: what are we counting as important other than our income and financial net worth? What are we accepting as inputs, and what feedback loops of new information can we add? What processes are consuming our time and energy? How much time, energy and capital do we have left to invest in changing our lives for the better? If we have little or no time and energy to invest, then that suggests a course of action: critically examine our priorities and our life as a system and figure out what can be modified to free up enough time, energy and capital to make the kind of progress we want to make.

Making these kinds of assessments is difficult, and writing them down helps put them in perspective. Looking at the list objectively—for example, as if it were a friend's— can also clarify our priorities and the tradeoffs we're making.

As part of the exercise of describing our life as a system, we can ask some basic questions:

What's our return if we invest nothing? All else being equal, the answer is generally "nothing."

What's our return if we gamble in a rigged game? Once again, the answer is typically "nothing."

What if we invest in unfavorable conditions and locales? In general, the yields will be limited by the fragility, unsustainability, inflexibility, autocracy, lack of diversity, agency and opportunity, and high costs of a locale that doesn't treat the capital of non-elites well.

What if we invest in forms of capital that don't mean much to us but we believe mean a lot to others? If we're not making progress on accumulating capital that's meaningful to us, the return will be unsatisfactory and unfulfilling.

How do we navigate the unsustainability and perverse incentives of the current economy? One answer is to control as much our capital as we can. If we rely on resources, income and decisions made a half-world away, we are vulnerable to disruptions that we can't control, and our dependence leaves us few options to re-establish control.

There are no risk-free options or perfect tradeoffs. What we can do is seek a localized, decentralized economy that is more like the sustainable, frugal, efficient, adaptable, self-organizing system described in Section Six, an economy that is reducing its dependence on the corrupt, wasteful, autocratic, centralized system that is careening toward the cliff of insolvency and dissolution. We need a local economy that welcomes us and our capital and treats us well enough that we want to stay because we're able to make progress on what matters most to us.

Charles Hugh Smith